Hampshire
& the New Forest
A DOG WALKER'S GUIDE

Vicky Fletcher

COUNTRYSIDE BOOKS
NEWBURY BERKSHIRE

First published 2011
Reprinted 2014, 2016
Updated and reprinted 2018, 2023
© Vicky Fletcher 2011

All rights reserved. No reproduction
permitted without the prior permission
of the publisher:

COUNTRYSIDE BOOKS
3 Catherine Road
Newbury, Berkshire

To view our complete range of books,
please visit us at
www.countrysidebooks.co.uk

ISBN 978 1 84674 233 0

Photographs by the author

Cover photograph supplied by
Roger Evans

All materials used in the manufacture of this book carry FSC certification.

Designed by Peter Davies, Nautilus Design
Produced through The Letterworks Ltd., Reading
Printed by The Holywell Press Ltd., Oxford

Contents

Introduction 5
Acknowledgements 5
🐾 Advice for Dog Walkers 6

Walk

1	Yateley Common *(3 miles)*	9
2	The Basingstoke Canal *(3 miles)*	13
3	Watership Down from Ecchinswell *(2 miles)*	17
4	St Mary Bourne *(5 miles)*	21
5	Houghton Droves *(3½ miles)*	26
6	The Mottisfont Estate *(3½ miles)*	30
7	River Itchen and Shawford Down *(2½ miles)*	35
8	New Alresford *(4½ miles)*	40
9	Old Winchester Hill *(6 miles)*	44
10	Hawkley's Hangers *(4 miles)*	48
11	Ludshott Common & Grayshott *(1 or 4½ miles)*	52
12	North Hayling *(4 miles)*	57
13	Titchfield to the Solent *(5½ miles)*	62
14	River Hamble Country Park *(3½ miles)*	66
15	Lepe Loop *(4½ miles)*	70
16	Barton Explorer *(2 miles)*	74
17	Rhinefield to Wilverley Plain *(5 miles)*	77
18	Smugglers' Road *(2½ miles)*	81
19	Fritham *(6 or 1½ miles)*	85
20	Breamore and the Miz-maze *(3½ miles)*	90

Appendix

🐾 Contact details for veterinary practices close to the walks 95

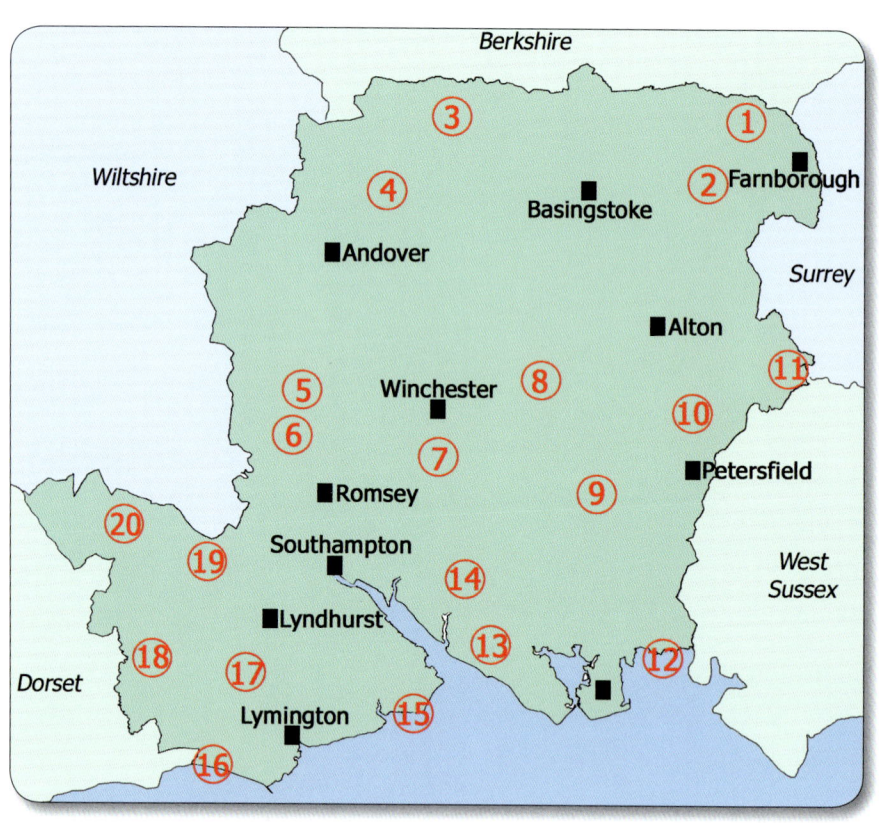

Area map showing location of the walks.

INTRODUCTION

In my family, Sundays were always about going for walks with our lively collie cross, Fagin. Somehow or other, the stresses and strains of the week would fall away as the five of us set out, sometimes for a local amble, sometimes armed with walking books to explore the countryside further afield. Some of our best memories are still about these walks, which gave us relaxed family time, plenty of fun and fresh air, and some great picnics and pub lunches. Fagin, of course, was always the centre of attention, enthusiastically chasing balls, leaping into water at every given opportunity, and making plenty of doggie friends. We still have a whole circle of friends and acquaintances we have met on various walks around our home, based on dogs and dog walking!

Since Fagin we have had a variety of rescue dogs, and so know only too well that every dog is definitely different! We have had some 'interesting' walks on routes we didn't know. We often had to lift the large, aging and often muddy Kelly over stiles, whilst making sure that the excitable JC didn't hurl herself into roads and barbed wire. Fagin was a one-dog disaster zone when it came to sheep, always trying to escape the lead the moment he smelt them, whereas poor little Ermintrude was petrified of all livestock. Turning up to a pub with dogs can also be a bit hit and miss. Some landlords we know always have water bowls and a kind word (sometimes even a biscuit or two) whereas others can be much less welcoming.

So that's where this book comes in handy. Hampshire and the New Forest is beautiful dog walking country, with lots of places to explore: from pretty chalk rivers and rolling downlands to ancient woodlands and, of course, the lovely Solent coastline. This book presents carefully selected walks from across the county, where stiles are kept to a minimum, and details of livestock encounters and other potential hazards are clear. Also included are details of cafés or pubs where dogs are welcome.

Happy walking!

Vicky Fletcher

Acknowledgements

Particular thanks go to Rob and my family, and to Michelle and Spike, Tim and Django, Nicky and Poppy, who accompanied me on my walks, and the many members of the Hampshire 20s and 30s Walking Group.

Hampshire & the New Forest

ADVICE FOR DOG WALKERS

The Countryside Code is the best place to start when understanding how to enjoy the countryside with your dog. This is a government publication providing advice and guidance for visitors to the countryside. It was updated in 2021 with clear advice for dog walkers (see links section below for website).

Key Countryside Code messages for dog owners include:

"Keep your dog under effective control to make sure it stays away from wildlife, livestock, horses and other people unless invited. You should:

- **always keep your dog on a lead or in sight**
- **be confident your dog will return on command**
- **make sure your dog does not stray from the path or area where you have right of access**

Always check local signs as there are situations when you must keep your dog on a lead for all or part of the year. It is good practice wherever you are to keep your dog on a lead around livestock.

Always clean up your dog's poo because it can cause illness in people, livestock and wildlife. Never leave bags of dog poo around. If you cannot find a public waste bin, you should take it home and use your own bin."

Dog walking in Hampshire

Livestock may be encountered along several of the walks in this book, with warnings given within the walks where possible.

Sheep and lambs will typically move away from dogs. Some dogs, like Fagin, love to chase sheep, but this can cause injury and cause lambs to abort (January to April is usually lambing time). Livestock owners are entitled by law to shoot dogs worrying livestock. If your dog is like Fagin, please do think ahead and put them on a lead in plenty of time.

Find the safest route around cattle and give them plenty of space. Cows are inquisitive by nature so may move towards you and your dog. This can be quite scary, but it is important to keep your nerve and continue walking slowly and calmly. On the rare occasions where cows behave aggressively drop the dog lead. This is safer for both you and the dog, as the dog can run away from the cattle and you can exit the area calmly and safely.

New Forest ponies are gentle in nature and normally ignore people and dogs. As with all other livestock please don't let your dog frighten or chase the ponies. Deer also have a strong scent, which can arouse a dog's hunting instincts. Pregnant females and young fawns are particularly vulnerable in spring and early summer.

Advice for Dog Walkers

Local Byelaws and Open Access Land
Do observe any local signs, notices and byelaws.
Byelaws apply in the New Forest. Some car parks are also subject to localised closure - the ones used in this book are currently all open year round. Do keep well away from any countryside work taking place.

Between 1 March and 31 July, it is a legal requirement to have your dog on a lead on open access land to help protect ground nesting birds, even if there is no livestock on the land. Walks that pass through open access land in this book include Yateley Common, Ludshott Common, Shawford Down, Old Winchester Hill, Barton, Rhinefield to Wilverley Plain, Smugglers Road and Fritham.

Adders, Ticks and Lyme Disease
Adders are present in Hampshire, and prefer rough, open countryside like heathland, and woodland-edge habitats. They normally stay well away from people and dogs, and never attack deliberately. If you are lucky enough to spot one, please do leave it alone. Dogs very occasionally get bitten when exploring due to their curious nature. If you suspect an adder bite take your dog to a vet immediately as the effects can be fatal if not treated, particularly for small dogs.

Ticks are common in the New Forest and other parts of rural Hampshire. They are tiny bloodsucking spider-like creatures, dark brown or black in colour and are often found in long grass, bracken and heather. If you brush past vegetation containing ticks they can bite both dogs and people. They can cause unpleasant skin reactions and lumps that can become infected and sore. Ticks can also carry Lyme disease which is more serious and also affects both dogs and people.

Vets can advise on any preventative products for your dog, such as vaccinations and 'spot on' repellents. Chemists can also provide advice on products for people, including some insect repellents. You can reduce the chance of a tick bite by wearing shoes rather than sandals, long trousers tucked into socks, and long-sleeved shirts. Light coloured clothing helps you to see ticks better. Always check yourself, your clothes, and your dog at the end of a walk. Ticks are easy to brush off as long as they haven't attached themselves.

If you or your dog does get bitten by a tick, they are best removed immediately as this reduces the likelihood of transmitting Lyme disease. Do check online for the best ways to remove a tick if needed.

The symptoms of Lyme disease are generally flu-like to begin, but can have serious complications if not treated. There may also be a distinctive rash, often described as looking like a bullseye on a dart board.

There have also been confirmed cases of Alabama Rot and Seasonal Canine Illness in Hampshire. Both are fortunately very rare.

Hampshire & the New Forest

Links and Further information
The Countryside Code:
www.gov.uk/government/publications/the-countryside-code.
Hampshire County Council – information on walks, places and spaces to visit, and 'countryside canines' – visiting the countryside with your dog:
www.hants.gov.uk/thingstodo/countryside
Forestry England – advice on dog health, including links to further information on ticks, seasonal canine illness and alabama rot:
www.forestryengland.uk/dog-health
New Forest dog walking information and guidance:
www.newforestnpa.gov.uk/things-to-do/walking/dog-walking
Just a tick information leaflet:
www.newforest.gov.uk/article/1363/Health-promotion
Insect bites and stings – Treatment:
https://www.nhs.uk/conditions/insect-bites-and-stings/treatment
UK Public Health advice:
ukhsa.blog.gov.uk/2014/03/24/tips-and-tricks-to-stay-safe-from-ticks
Alabama Rot: www.vets4pets.com/pet-health-advice/alabama-rot
....

PUBLISHER'S NOTE

We hope that you obtain considerable enjoyment from this book. Although at the time of publication all routes followed public rights of way or permitted paths, diversion orders can be made and permissions withdrawn.

   We cannot, of course, be held responsible for such diversion orders and any inaccuracies in the text which result from these or any other changes to the routes, nor any damage which might result from walkers trespassing on private property. We are anxious though that all details covering the walks are kept up to date and would therefore welcome information from readers which would be relevant to future editions.

   The simple sketch maps that accompany the walks in the book are based on notes made by the author whilst checking out the routes on the ground. For the benefit of a proper map, however, we do recommend that you purchase the relevant Ordnance Survey sheet covering your walk. The Ordnance Survey maps are widely available, especially through booksellers and local newsagents.

Yateley Common

Reflections in Wyndham's Pool.

This figure of eight circuit dips in and out of heathland and woodland, allowing dogs to roam off the lead along bridleways, and there are plenty of shallow ponds along the route for water-loving dogs to cool off in. Just 5 minutes from the M3 in the midst of busy north east Hampshire, this gently undulating walk offers a surprisingly peaceful walk with colourful views over brown and purple heaths, birch and pine woods, and large tranquil ponds.

Terrain

Terrain is relatively gentle, with a few ups and downs along the route but no steep climbs, and there are benches at all three ponds for a rest (or a canine swim!). Most of the pathways in and around the common are well-marked wide bridleways. There is normally good visibility though for dog owners and horse riders to see each other coming, and plenty of space to pass without fuss. Stout footwear is a must in winter-time or when there has been heavy rain as horses can churn the bridleways up into thick mud in a few hotspots,

Hampshire & the New Forest

particularly around Cottage Farm. The route occasionally leaves these wide tracks to go onto well-used footpaths through woodland and heathland. There are also a few hundred yards or so along tarmac or dirt-tracks where cars could be encountered (moving very slowly over the potholes). These tracks are not on the main road network but provide access for the lucky residents of the handful of heathland cottages passed on the route.

Where to park
The free car-park off Cricket Hill Lane, Yateley (GR: SU822597). Be sure to take the left hand fork to the carpark - the right hand lane leads to a small row of cottages with limited turning places. **OS map:** Explorer 145 Guildford and Farnham.

How to get there:
Yateley Common is just off the A30 between Yateley and Blackwater. Exit the M3 at Junction 4a, and take the A327, following signs for Reading (A327) Blackwater (A30) and Yateley. At the junction of the A327 and the A30, go straight over the roundabout (2nd Exit), taking a b-road signposted Yateley and Cricket Hill. On entering Yateley look out to the right for a row of houses, and turn right into a lane by the sign-board for Yateley Common.

Nearest refreshments
There are two pubs within a few minutes' drive. The Cricketers in Cricket Hill Lane, Yateley ☎ 01252872105 and the Ely Hotel on the A30 ☎ 01252 860444. Both serve food and allow well behaved dogs in the bar areas.

Dog factors
Distance: 3 miles
Road walking: 1/4 mile along quiet tracks; crosses near to two small on site car-parks. The busy A30 runs within 100 yards on one stretch of the route.
Livestock: Possibility of encountering horse riders along the route. The route also passes near to fenced-off pony paddocks in some places.
Stiles: None
Nearest Vets: Kynoch Vets (Medivet Yateley), or Firgrove Veterinary Centre, both in Yateley.

Yateley Common 1

The Walk

1. From the car park follow the steps down to **Wyndham's Pool**. With the water on your right follow the bridleway into wooded heathland, and then take the right hand fork up a slight slope. Continue across to the small cemetery and parking area straight ahead.

2. Turn right and take the narrow path immediately to the left, following the cemetery boundary. As the path bends slightly to the right take the left hand fork, joining a bridleway. The view opens up onto pony paddocks to the left and right. On emerging onto a tarmaced track, follow the bridleway to the right past **Cottage** and **Follyfoot Farms** through woodland to re-enter **Yateley Common**. Here you come to an area where several paths meet and the woodland emerges into heathland again.

3. Continue straight on to **Stroud Pond**, a scenic pond area and a delightful spot to picnic with a shallow swimming place for any water loving dog. You will also return to this spot on the return leg of your figure of eight so you could take a short-cut back to the start point from here. To continue, with the pond on your right-hand side take the left-hand fork up a gentle slope with a holly-bush boundary line to the left and continue straight on. At the top of the slope turn left down a bridleway, past **The Hollies** and two other houses

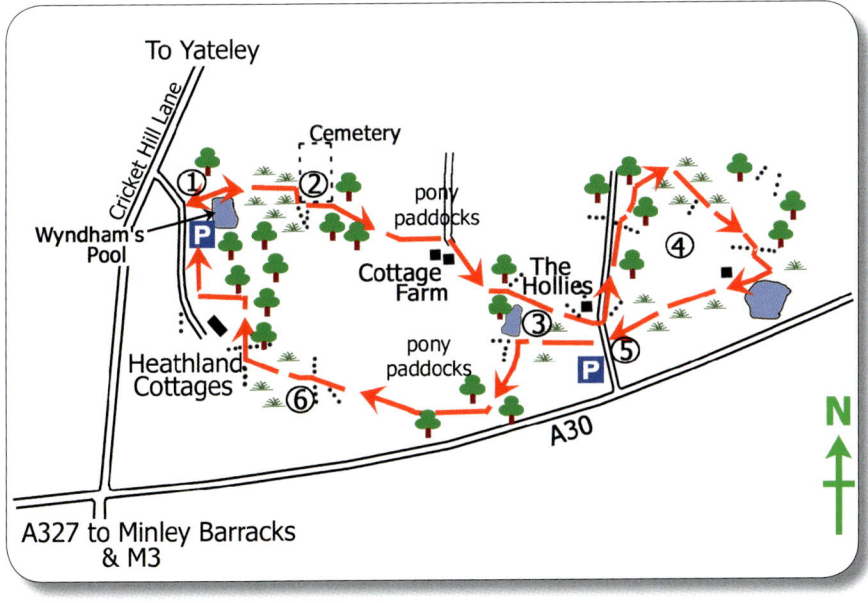

11

Hampshire & the New Forest

to your left. Opposite the fourth property (**Heathfields**), take the right hand bridleway through woodland to re-enter Yateley Common. Take the woodland pathway to the left, emerging onto open heath. Ignoring smaller pathways joining to the left, keep following the path as it bends to the right.

4 At a meeting of several paths on the heath keep following the bridleway sign along a left-hand fork, cross a wide track and continue straight on along a narrower pathway with a slight slope up through the heathland. Continue until the path crosses a further wide bridleway and turn right following the track through birch trees to a grassy area and a large pond. Cross to the pond, especially if your dog loves water, but bear in mind that the busy A30 is potentially within reach for more adventurous dogs who like to run off. Keeping the water to your left pass **Haywards Cottage** to the right, keeping to the left-hand fork of the bridleway through gorsey heathland. After 500 yards this crosses a tarmac lane (**Stroud Lane**), with a parking area to the left.

5 You will be able to see **The Hollies** again down a bridleway to the right. Continue straight on down a wooded track which skirts the car park to your left. You now re-enter the open heathland. Continue down the hill to re-join **Stroud Pond**. For the final leg of the figure of eight, turn your back on the pond and with the pony paddocks to the right follow the bridleway up a slight slope, skirting round the grassy enclosure into woodland. *The busy A30 runs close by this pathway again for a few hundred yards here.* At the top of the slope the woodland opens out onto a heathland plateau. Take the right-hand fork in tracks here, and after 300 yards or so you will come to a junction of pathways with power lines also meeting over-head.

6 Turn right here, down a bridleway through the heathland. At a T-junction of bridleways turn left continuing down to the bottom of the hill and continue straight on across a further bridleway going back up hill. Turn right after 80 yards or so towards a row of houses. Continue along the bridleway and access track with the houses on your right-hand side back to **Wyndham's Pool** and the car park. There is also a parallel woodland path to the right-hand side if preferred.

Gorse on Yateley Common.

The Basingstoke Canal

The towpath just before Tundry Pond.

This pretty circular walk is charming in all seasons, centred around a long loop of the canal lined by woodland along much of the route, which provides shade in summer and is beautiful in winter frosts. Dogs can go off the lead along the canal towpaths, although there are some sections where you may want to keep more adventurous dogs close by you. There are also occasional spots en route where the towpaths dip and water-loving dogs can swim in the still canal waters. The wildlife, old bridges, occasional quaint canalside houses and Dogmersfield Park also provide interest along the way for dog walkers.

Terrain
A flat walk, mainly on well-surfaced canal towpaths, with occasional slight inclines onto bridges over the canal. The canal loop is connected by public

Hampshire & the New Forest

footpaths through a rural estate, mainly on grassy paths along the shores of Tundry Pond, and on metalled tracks through Dogmersfield Park estate. There are very occasional patches that could be muddy in wet weather or winter. The towpaths however, remain nice and firm in winter, making this a good all-weather route.

Where to park
Basingstoke Canal free car park on Sprats Hatch Lane, located opposite the Barley Mow pub (GR: SU778537). The car park also has a dog poo bin.
OS map: Explorer 144 Basingstoke, Alton & Whitchurch.

How to get there
Winchfield Hurst lies between Fleet and Hook, 10 minutes from junction 5 of the M3. Take the B3349 north towards Mattingley, then turn right onto the A30 towards Yateley and Camberley, and right again onto the B3016 to Odiham. After passing under the M3 turn left following signs for Winchfield station. Winchfield Hurst lies around 1½ miles further on from the station towards Dogmersfield. On spotting the Barley Mow look out for Sprats Hatch Lane opposite the pub. The canal car park is on the left. The village can also be reached from the A287 or B3013 – follow signs for Dogmersfield and then Winchfield station from Dogmersfield. Sat Nav: RG27 8DE

Nearest refreshments
There is a canalside picnic table near to the car park. The Barley Mow is just opposite the car park, does food and is dog friendly. Dogs are permitted in the main bar, lounge bar and garden. www.barley-mow.com. ☎ 01252 617490.

Dog factors
Distance: 3 miles.
Road walking: None.
Livestock: Possibility of sheep and cattle between points 2 and 3, and horses at point 4, but behind sturdy wire fences.
Stiles: 1 stile, with gaps to the side, which dogs of labrador size or less will easily get through (except less agile or very wide dogs).
Cyclists: The route is popular with cyclists, particularly families and leisure cyclists, so you will need to share the towpath.
Nearest vets: Ashworth Veterinary Group or Ark Veterinary Group, both in Fleet.

The Basingstoke Canal

The Walk

1 With your back to the car park, walk up the slight incline onto the canal towpath, and turn left, keeping the canal on your right. *Dogs can go off the lead along the towpath, but there is a rural road running parallel to the path for the first 200 yards or so beyond the trees, which my brother's lively dog, on loan to me for the weekend, managed to find her way onto immediately.* Continue on the towpath for just over a mile until **Tundry Pond** (more of a lake) starts to stretch out to the right beyond the canal and **Blacksmith's Bridge** lies ahead.

The canal was completed in 1794 to transport agricultural products from Basingstoke to London, taking us back to the days before cars and railways when the pace of life was certainly much slower. Restoration started in the 1970s and today over 30 miles of permissive pathways along the tranquil canal have been restored, almost from Basingstoke itself to the River Wey Navigation in Surrey. Much of the canal is a Site of Special Scientific Interest with exceptional wildlife interest, particularly dragonflies in early summer.

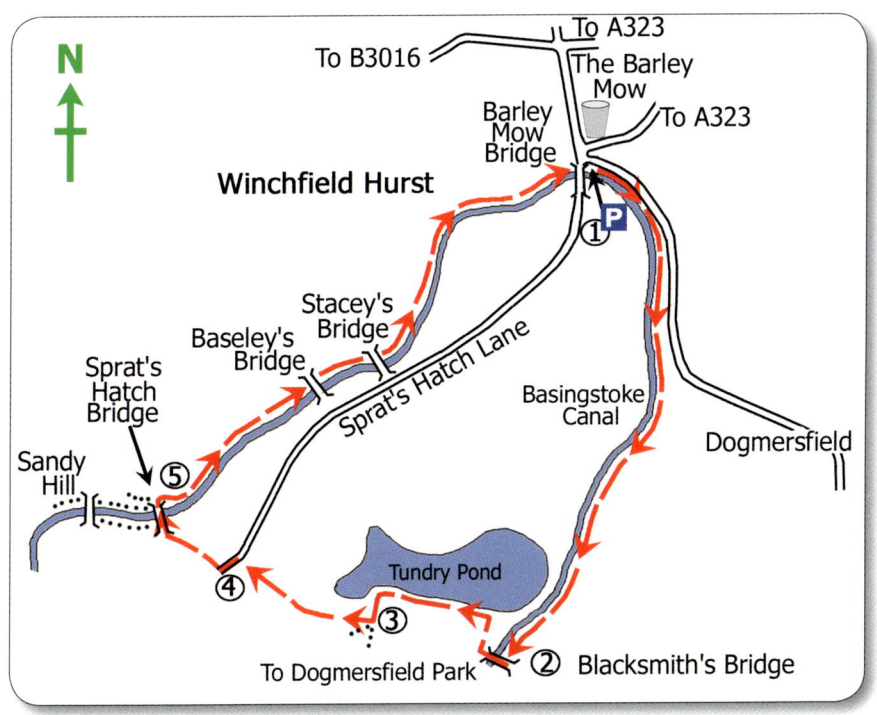

Hampshire & the New Forest

2 Rather than passing under Blacksmith's Bridge, climb up the short slope to the bridge and cross over the canal. There is one fairly sturdy stile ahead, with small/medium dog-sized gaps to the side. Turn right, then follow the path around to the left along the shores of **Tundry Pond** lake (do bear in mind this is a private fishing lake, so your dog may not be welcome in the water).

3 On reaching a fenceline, with a bridge crossing the lake to the right, turn left through the metal kissing gate and up the gravel path, looking towards **Dogmersfield House and Park** in the distance. There is likely to be livestock (sheep and cattle) in the fields of the park, although behind sturdy fences. After 50 yards, at a set of gates, take the lower of two signposted footpaths (the right-hand fork) along the metalled track, keeping views of the lake to the right. After a further 50 yards, follow the signposted footpath to the right of more gates, leading between the fields to a kissing gate.

The grandiose Dogmersfield House was built in 1728. It was added to and restored in the 1980s, and is now a Four Seasons Hotel. It stands on the site of a much older property, to which Henry VI was a frequent visitor.

4 You will now be re-joined by Sprats Hatch Lane from the right *but dogs don't necessarily need to go back on the lead as it is here a quiet metalled access track for just a handful of properties.* Turn left down the track (a marked bridleway), keeping the houses to your right. The pathway bends around to the right, between two pony paddocks (again, well fenced) to re-join the canal and Sprats Hatch Bridge. Cross over the canal and turn right down onto the towpath. This is an important junction otherwise you could end up a long way from the start point!

5 Continue along the towpath, checking that the canal is to your right. Pass under **Baseley's Bridge** and **Stacey's Bridge** after ½ mile or so, and continue back to **Barley Mow Bridge** and the car park.

Springtime on the Basingstoke Canal.

Watership Down from Ecchinswell

Looking over Watership Down.

A short countryside loop taking in views of the dramatic chalk scarp of Watership Down made famous by the novel of the same name written by local author Richard Adams. Dogs can go off the leads for much of the walk on the old drovers' tracks to happily sample the tantalising smells and dream of bunnies themselves. The countryside here is part of the North Wessex Downs Area of Outstanding Natural Beauty, and the peace and quiet of this lovely rural area cannot help but charm. The AONB is known for its chalk hills, and dramatic scarps and valleys, but this route presents a relatively gentle climb using bridleways, footpaths and rural village lanes, allowing you to take in the views of steeper countryside around and about without having to climb it. A lovely walk all year that leaves behind the hustle and bustle of modern life. The pretty Royal Oak in Ecchinswell also awaits on your return.

Hampshire & the New Forest

Dog factors
Distance: 2 miles.
Road walking: There is ¼ to ½ mile on quiet rural village lanes.
Livestock: None directly on the route, but there are sheep in some of the adjacent fields and the walk passes through farmland, so you will need to keep dogs under control throughout the walk.
Stiles: 3 between points 1 and 2. These all have open areas underneath or to the side, which all medium-sized dogs and under should be able to use, but there is an alternative route through the village for less agile breeds (or owners)
Nearest vets: GKG Vets, Kingsclere and Newbury.

Terrain
Mostly uses old drove tracks – wide grassy footpaths lined by hedgerows passing in between the fields. Some road walking through the village and on quiet lanes with little through traffic. Surfaces are mainly good, but the footpaths may be a little slippery or muddy in winter. You will certainly feel the climb to Nuthanger Farm and the return ascent, but it is a gentle and steady one, and the views from the top well worth it.

Where to park
On street in the village but please be considerate to residents. There is also public parking opposite the school (GR: SU500596). **OS map:** Explorer 144 Basingstoke, Alton & Whitchurch.

How to get there
Ecchinswell lies between the A34 and the A339. If approaching from the north or from the Basingstoke direction, follow the A339; the village is signposted at several points from the A339. If you are approaching on the A34 from the south, exit at the junction signposted for Beacon Hill and Burghclere. Turn right, back under the A34, pass through Old Burghclere and Sydmonton, and then follow signs left towards Ecchinswell. Sat Nav: RG20 4UA

Nearest refreshments
The Royal Oak is a welcoming village pub with an extensive beer garden running down to the stream, and home-made food. Well-behaved dogs welcome. Website: www.royaloakecchinswell.co.uk ☎ 01635 297355.

Watership Down from Ecchinswell   3

The Walk

1 With the school in front of you, turn right along the road. If you wish to avoid the stiles, follow route 1a which continues along the road, turning left before the village pub (signposted '**Kingsclere**'). Cross a charming stream and follow the road round to the left climbing slightly until you come to **Clere**

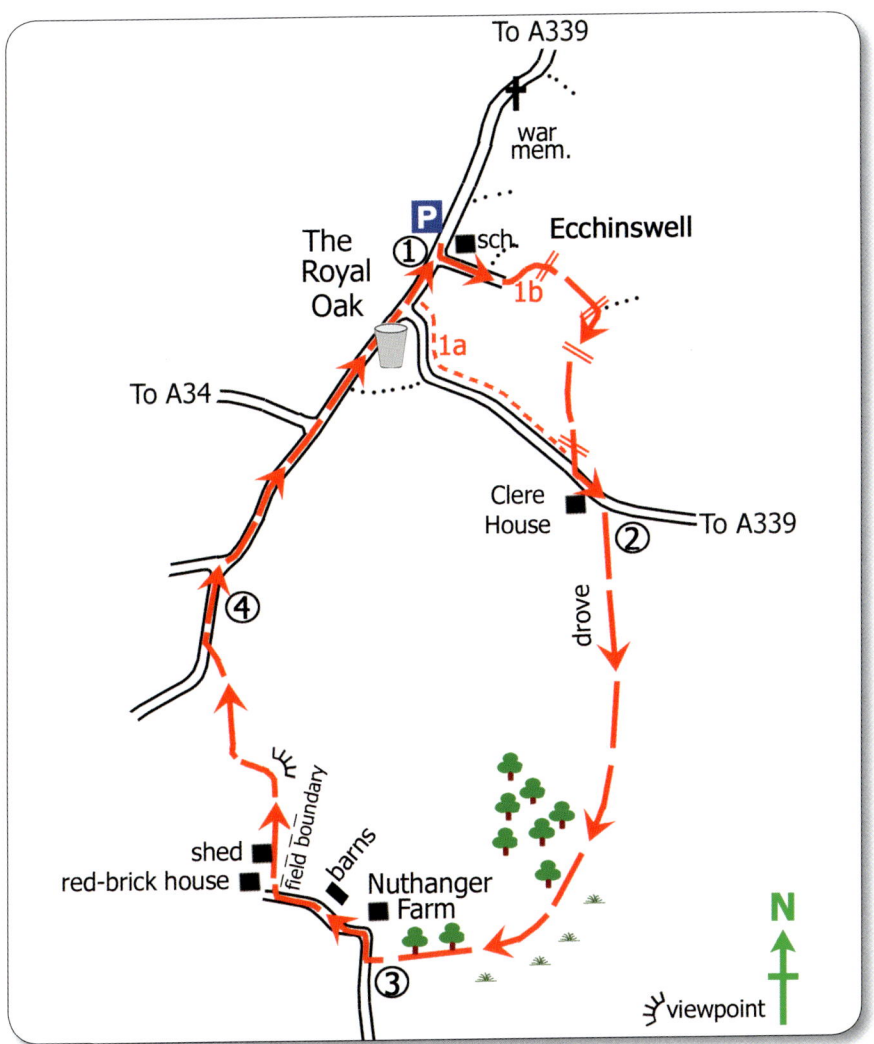

Hampshire & the New Forest

The drove at point 2 of the route.

House on the right. Pass the house to a footpath on the right-hand side. The roads are not busy, but you will probably need to keep your dog on a lead as you may encounter the occasional car.

For the off road route (1b), with three stiles, turn left down **Mill Lane** just after the school. At the end of the housing continue straight on, past the gates of **Elderfield**. The footpath takes you left to the side of the property, through a kissing gate and then, passing between fields, to stile 1. Turn right, keeping to the field margin, and cross stile 2. Cross the grass to stile 3 at the top left corner of the field. Cross over the road, and turn left past **Clere House** to the footpath on the right.

❷ Follow the drove gently up the side of the valley, looking out onto the downlands. Eventually as you follow the path to the right you will be able to see the majestic scarp of **Watership Down** across on the other side of the valley and the path stops rising. Keep on along the path, enjoying the views to the left, until you come to a junction with a metalled track at the end of the field. *Dogs should be on leads through the farm, and under control through the farmland.*

❸ Turn right along the track towards **Nuthanger Farm**, then left before the gates, following the metalled road past barns on the right towards a lone red-brick house. Turn right before this property, and keep to the right-hand bank. The footpath is not marked here but have confidence – it runs alongside the field bank, to the right of the outbuildings, and soon broadens out, descending back down through farmland with nice views over Ecchinswell.

❹ As the path joins the road, keep going straight on, soon reaching the first houses of the village, and the welcome sign of the **Royal Oak**. After suitable refreshment, continue straight on back to the car.

St Mary Bourne

One of the three dog-friendly stiles on the route.

Nestled in the hills of the North Wessex Downs Area of Outstanding Natural Beauty, St Mary Bourne is a picturesque village stretched along the Bourne Rivulet, a tributary of the River Test. Dogs can go off leads on drovers' lanes, and will enjoy the rural smells and a good stretch of the legs. The village welcomes walking visitors, and a lot of care has been taken to make routes dog-friendly. A working and very rural historic landscape, this walk takes you deep into the downlands, a patchwork of fields, often following old drovers' routes. There is evidence that these chalk downlands have been farmed since Neolithic times, with successive generations modifying the landscape ever since, and some of the modern settlements dating to the early medieval or even Saxon era. The village is also known for its watercress, and its beds are commercially run.

Hampshire & the New Forest

Dog factors

Distance: 5 miles
Road walking: ½ mile along very quiet rural lanes; the route crosses the busy village road in two places.
Livestock: Possibility of sheep between points 2 and 3, and beyond the drovers' track between 6 and 7.
Stiles: 3 – all well maintained with special dog flaps.
Nearest vets: Foxcotte Veterinary Group, Whitchurch.

Terrain

A gently undulating walk, with no very steep climbs or descents. The route is mainly on footpaths and farm tracks, with some road walking on quiet lanes. Many of the paths skirt field edges, so may be muddy in winter. Despite its very rectangular shape, the walk is not as easy to navigate as it looks, but is well signposted with orange waymarkers.

Where to park

The free parish car park opposite the George pub, backing onto the recreation ground and the village shop (GR: SU422504). **OS map:** Explorer 144 Basingstoke, Alton & Whitchurch.

How to get there

St Mary Bourne lies on the B3048. This can be accessed directly from the A303, or from the B3400 which runs between Whitchurch and Andover. If approaching from the A34, exit at the Whitchurch turn-off, drive into the village, and pick up the B3400 from there. Sat Nav: SP11 6BG

Nearest refreshments

The George Inn sits in the heart of the village and welcomes walkers and dogs (☎ 01264 738153; www.georgeinnstmarybourne.co.uk). Alternatively the Bourne Valley Inn (☎ 01264 738361; www.bournevalleyinn.com) lies ½ mile south of the village. This is an old coaching inn with an extensive menu from sandwiches to specials.

The Walk

1 With dogs on leads, exit the car park past the shop and community centre out onto the main road. Taking great care of traffic, cross over the road towards the **George pub**, then turn left into **Spring Mill Lane**. After 100 yards or

St Mary Bourne 4

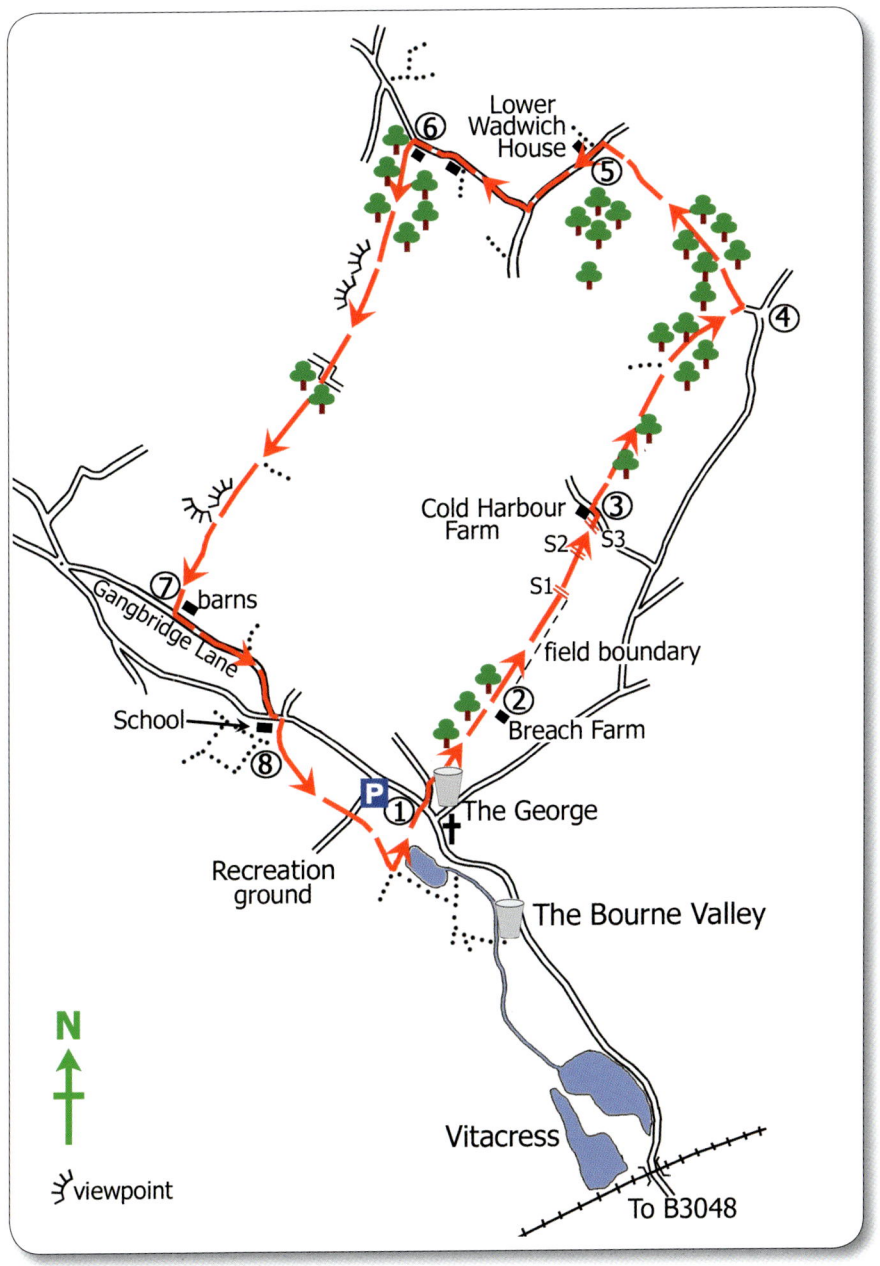

Hampshire & the New Forest

so, look out for **Hirst and Sons**, a small industrial unit up a steep driveway. Take the footpath signposted to the right-hand side of the driveway, following orange markers, up some steps and to the side of Hirst and Sons. This widens out into a gravel driveway lined by trees and hedges.

2 When the driveway stops at a farm, continue straight on, following the orange markers, alongside a long arable field, keeping the field boundary to your right, to stile 1 in the corner of the field. Continue straight through the next pasture field (sheep may be present here) to stile 2, and again straight across the next field towards **Cold Harbour Farm** and stile 3.

3 Turn left into a quiet lane, then opposite the farmhouse turn right back into the fields through a large gap in the hedge. Continue straight on along the field margins through two smaller fields and a large field (connected by gaps not stiles), then the path passes between two large hedges. At the next field boundary continue through the gap, and diagonally across the field on a mown path, aiming for a house at the bottom of the hill. Pass through another gap onto a wooded farm track.

4 Turn left onto the track and through the woodlands, emerging again into fields. Continue straight on until you see the roof of a large modern red-brick house, and continue down to the road – **Wadwick Bottom**.

5 Turn left into the road past the large house, *with dogs on leads if you prefer (it is a very quiet road, serving local farms and houses)*. At the fork take the right-hand lane, and continue on past a large field and two dwellings. Just after the second house, as the road bends round and goes downhill, look out for a signposted footpath on the left.

6 Continue along the straight tree-lined ancient track for ½ mile or so, enjoying the views down the valley through the trees, and again as the path opens up with views across the fields. The route is then crossed by a farm track and enters a narrow tree-lined pathway, and goes out into an arable field. Pass around the field boundary. At the end of the field our route leaves the orange waymarkers, and continues straight on down the drove track towards the village. In the farmyard at the bottom of the hill, pass to the right of the large barns to a gap in the bottom corner, and *with dogs on leads* exit onto **Gangbridge Lane**.

7 Turn left down the lane, past plenty of picturesque houses towards the village. At the junction with the main village through-road take particular care with your dogs and cross over to the school. The **Coronation Arms** is just a short distance further on if you care for liquid refreshments now. Proceed down

St Mary Bourne

School Lane to the left of the school, and through a decorated metal gate at the end, picking up the **Test Way.**

8 Follow the Test Way across the fields, through three further gates, across a lane, and through two further gates to the recreation ground and your car. If you have the energy, it is worth admiring the pond in the next field along, and also stopping at the local community-run shop before getting back into the car.

The route from School Lane to the recreation ground has been devised with help from local schoolchildren, and you can still see their poems on some of the gateposts. It provides a safe route to school away from the main village road, which is narrow and has no pavements in some areas.

The field path at point 2 of the walk.

Houghton Droves

Enjoying a paddle in the River Test.

An easy to navigate rectangular walk along old drove tracks on the downs. This is working farmland, but still a great walk for dogs with over half off the lead. A slight but steady climb up Faithfulls Drove gives views over the pretty chalk landscape of rolling hills, arable and livestock fields, and is rewarded by a shady green walk back down Stevens Drove. There is also the chance for a cool off and paddle at the end in the pretty River Test on summer days, perhaps while you enjoy a drink or picnic on the river bank. Houghton itself has a traditional rural feel, with quaint thatched cottages and, of course, a dog-friendly pub!

Houghton Droves 5

Terrain
Mostly on farm tracks and wide pathways, some surfaced; others can be muddy in wet weather. Undulating terrain, with a steady incline between points 1 and 2, which you will definitely feel, but no steep ups or downs.

Where to park
On-road parking in the gravel layby beside the footpath to the Test Way for four to five cars (GR: SU341318). Further off-road parking in the estates off Stevens Drove, but do make sure you are not a nuisance to residents. Patrons of the Boot Inn may be able to use the pub car park while they are walking.
OS map: Explorer 131 Romsey, Andover & Test Valley. For those who don't mind a longer walk (1½ miles each way) there is a large free public car park opposite the John O'Gaunt pub at Horsebridge (GR: SU345305), with a beautiful walk to Houghton along and across the River Test via the Monarch's Way and the Clarendon Way (no stiles).

How to get there
Houghton lies just off the A3057 between Romsey and Stockbridge. From Romsey follow the A3057 north and start looking out for the signposts just to the south of King's Somborne. You will cross the River Test via two road bridges just after the John O'Gaunt pub at Horsebridge (☎ 01794 388644), then turn right into the village. Houghton is also accessible via a minor road signposted from the western stretch of the long Stockbridge High Street (the A30), just to the west of the River Test. Sat Nav: SO20 6LP

Nearest refreshments
The Boot Inn, Houghton (www.thebootinn-houghton.co.uk; ☎ 01794 388310) is dog-friendly and serves food, with outdor areas on summer days, and the

Dog factors
Distance: 3½ miles.
Road walking: 300 yards through the village on a B road, with a pavement.
Livestock: Formerly known for its sheep, this part of the Hampshire Downs landscape now pays its way with arable and pig farming. There are free-range pigs behind electric fencing in one of the fields along the route, so dogs need to go on leads in some places.
Stiles: None.
Nearest vets: Walkabout Vet, Over Wallop; Mainstone Veterinary Clinic and Orchard Veterinary Clinic, both in Romsey.

Hampshire & the New Forest

patrons are used to walkers, cyclists, joggers, fishermen and those enjoying other country pursuits. The Boot Inn has tables overlooking the River Test.

The Walk

❶ Keeping to the pavement, turn left along the road and continue for 100 yards or so, then turn right into **Faithfulls Drove**, also signed as a footpath with a fingerpost. Continue up the road, and pass through the gap to the side of a gate as the road turns into a farm track. Pass a second gate, again with a gap to the side. The path steadily but gently rises, then undulates with a slight fall and rise.

There is likely to be livestock on either side of the path as this is a pig farming area, so dogs need to be under close control on the path. There are fences and hedgerows along much of the path, but occasional patches are open, with low electric fences. My dog for the day, the handsome Django, loves to roam and explore, so had to be kept on the lead here.

❷ After 1¼ miles along this track, coming down over a rise, you will start to see houses to the left. The farm track turns into a path along the side of an arable field, which dips down through a gap in the hedge and down some steps to

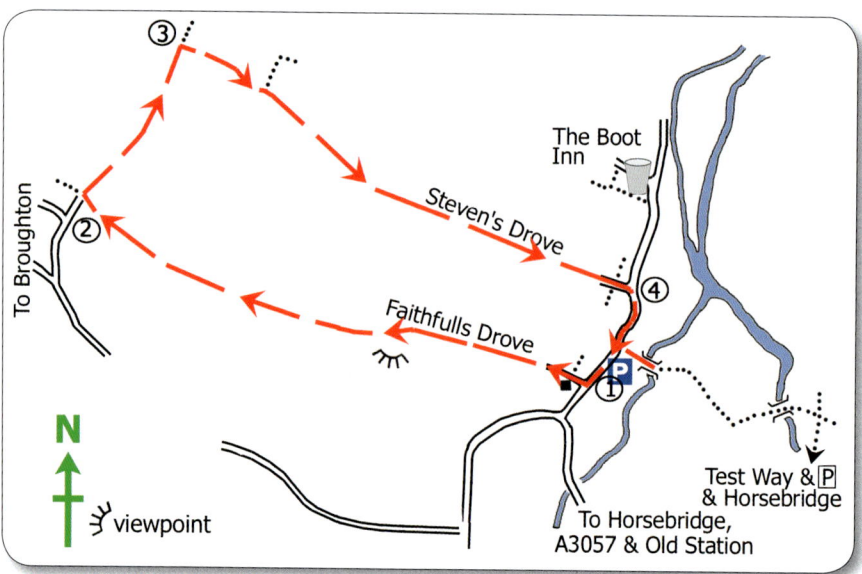

Houghton Droves 5

Looking across the pig farm near the start of the walk.

another footpath – an old drovers' track between fields. Turn right along the path and continue along it for ½ mile.

You should be able to let your dog off here, with arable fields on either side and no main roads nearby. Django was able to explore all the great smells along the path at his leisure.

3 Stop when you reach a gap in the hedgerow to the right and crossroads of paths, marked with a bench and some footpath signs. After you have re-gained your breath, turn right beside the field (ignoring the signposts that go straight on), which soon turns into another leafy green lane. Continue down the track (**Stevens Drove**) for another 1¼ miles, until you start to see the signs of a tarmac road and housing at the bottom of the track.

Django was happy off the lead all the way along the track; there may be livestock in the lower fields, but thick wooded hedgerows along both sides of the path kept him occupied. Dogs on the leads again when you start to reach the end of the drove.

4 Cross onto the pavement and continue past the housing estate to the Houghton road. Turn left for the **Boot Inn** – 300 yards away – or right for the car. Just before you reach the car there is a footpath signposted to the left. Less than 100 yards away, a shallow branch of the River Test flows past the end of the pathway and can be easily accessed by both dogs and owners for a paddle and cool down on warm days.

29

The Mottisfont Estate

A shady path in Spearywell Wood.

One of my all time Hampshire favourites, the Mottisfont Estate walk is a tranquil and rural idyll of well-cared for farmland, meadows, woodlands and copses, with a pub stop en route. Dogs can run free in the woodlands and meadows and can play in the River Dun. A lovely walk in all seasons, with bluebells in spring, wildflowers and shady spots to enjoy in summer, and crisp country views in winter. The walk starts in Spearywell Wood, and loops around gently undulating farmland to the River Dun, and takes in the villages of Dunbridge and Mottisfont on the return. Take time to enjoy wildlife in the woodlands, meadows and copses. The Spearywell woodlands are internationally important for their night-time occupants (bats!).

The Mottisfont Estate 6

Much of the land belongs to the estate of Mottisfont Abbey and House, run by the National Trust, although the abbey is not directly on the route. It is a paying attraction which is well worth visiting, particularly in June for stunning rose gardens. The original priory was founded in 1201 by William Briwere, a trusted adviser to Richard the Lionheart, King John and Henry III, and one of the barons who signed the Magna Carta. At the dissolution of the Monasteries the priory was converted to a house, transformed in the 18th Century and added to by successive generations.

Terrain
Certainly not a flat route, but the terrain is gently undulating rather than challenging. The walk uses well-surfaced paths through Spearywell Wood, then follows rights of way – mainly footpaths in good condition, which are waymarked.

Where to park
The free National Trust car park at Spearywell Wood (GR: SU315277). Signs and car park are visible from the B3084. **OS map:** Explorer 131 Romsey, Andover & Test Valley.

How to get there
Mottisfont lies between Romsey and Stockbridge close to both the A3057 and B3084, which run broadly parallel with each other on either side of the Test Valley. For an easy route follow signs for Mottisfont Abbey from the A3057 then continue past the Abbey entrance into

Dog factors
Distance: 3½ miles.
Road walking: The walk crosses a railway line and the B3084 around Dunbridge (end of point 4), and there is a section (a few hundred yards) on very quiet lanes and village roads around Mottisfont. There is also a 50-yard stretch on the B3084 at the end of the walk to return to the car park.
Livestock: None encountered, but the meadow may be grazed in the winter.
Stiles: 2 stiles between points 4 and 5 with gaps to the side, which all but very large dogs should be able to negotiate.
Nearest vets: Orchard Veterinary Surgery (Romsey centre) or Mainstone Veterinary Clinic (just south of Romsey on the A27).

Hampshire & the New Forest

Mottisfont village. After a sharp right corner in the village, turn left down the road signposted for Dunbridge and Broughton. Turn right onto the B3084 and watch out for the carpark on the left. Sat Nav SO51 0LS.

Nearest refreshments

The Mill Arms at Dunbridge is on the route and manages to be both smart yet welcoming to walkers and dogs, and does lovely food (☎ 01794 340355). Well-behaved dogs are welcome in the bar area.

The Walk

1 From the car park take the main wide track leading into the woodland straight ahead from the welcome board and gate, following signs for the **Mottisfont Estate Path**. Ignore a wide grassy ride to the right-hand side and, at a fork in paths, continue on the wide estate path along the right-hand fork. At an obvious T-junction of paths turn left, marked with a stone waymarker, continuing within the woodland. After 150 yards or so you will come to a woodland edge and a fork in paths. Take the right-hand path, still following the **Mottisfont Estate Path** downhill slightly into the woodland, with an open field visible to your left and continue for a further 200 yards.

2 At a meeting of five pathways, ignore the two paths to the right. Turn left and then immediately take the right-hand fork, leading down into the woodland with the arable field still visible to your left. As you descend to a second arable field, ignore a small path off to the left and bear round to the right.

3 At the next fork of the path, turn left out of the woodland and across a small bridge over a ditch into an arable field. Continue straight across the field following the clearly worn right of way to the hedgerow opposite and pass through a wide gap in the hedge to a meeting of two public footpaths. Continue along the public footpath straight ahead alongside thick hedgerow, keeping the hedgerow to your left.

The view of coppiced woodlands to the right opens up after a few minutes into fields. On reaching a woodland dell with several ditches bear right keeping to higher ground; continue along a wooded path between fields. Pass under a railway bridge. *You may want to call long-roaming dogs to heel close to this point due to a road not far ahead.*

4 Just before the **River Dun** turn left into a meadow through a kissing gate (though do pause to admire the river, have a paddle, and catch your breath first, bearing in mind the B road just over the bridge). Continue straight on through the beautiful meadow. The railway line is deceptively close, despite

The Mottisfont Estate 6

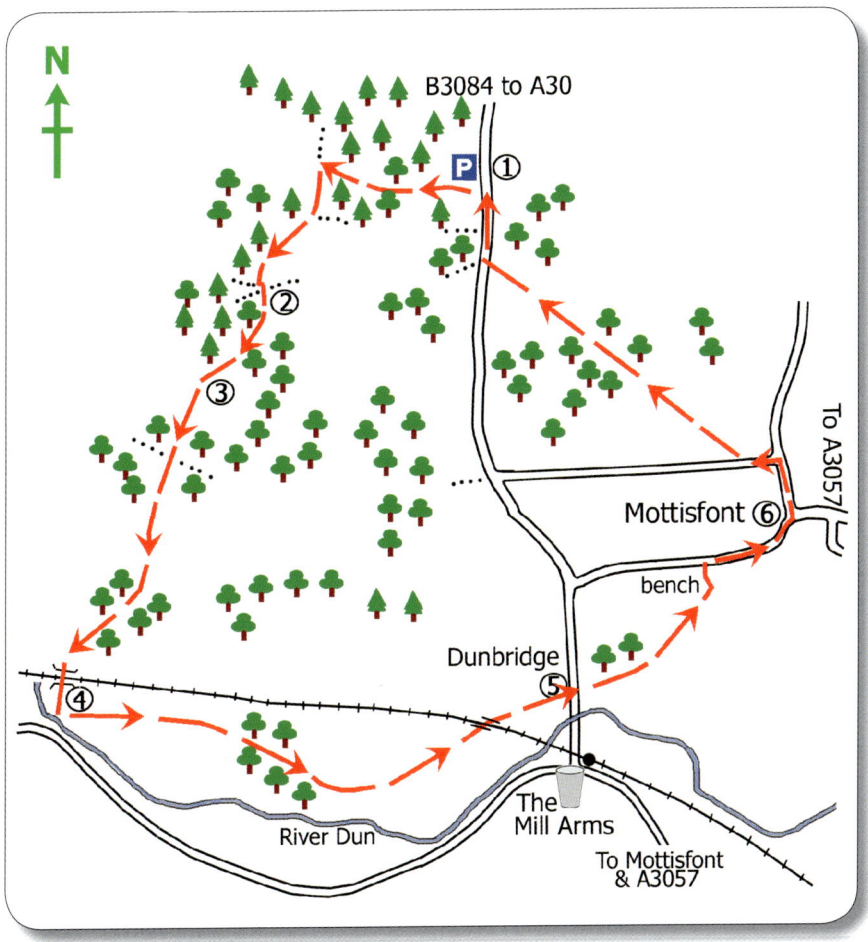

the tranquility of the meadow, so potentially accessible in places to very wide-roaming dogs. My dog for the day, the independent Django, found enough smells in the meadow to keep his attention.

You here come to the two stiles and a gate to pass through a small copse. *Both stiles have wide gaps for dogs of around 60cm which Django, a German Pointer, passed through without even breaking his stride.* The path continues past a field on the left up a slight incline to a wide gap in the hedgerow, and passes through a beautiful copse for a few hundred meters, emerging onto a farm track passing a small cottage. Continue up the track to the railway line.

Hampshire & the New Forest

This crossing is overground, and the kissing gate will not be much of a barrier for many dogs, so do put them on the lead early. Look and listen carefully for passing trains, and pass over the line, through the next kissing gate, and continue along the track. You may want to keep your dog on the lead as there is a road not far ahead.

5 Cross over the road, and through the kissing gate into the field. If you fancy a drink or food at this point **The Mill Arms** is only a few hundred meters to the right. Continue diagonally across the field up a gentle slope towards the clump of trees. Pass through a kissing gate and continue straight on across the next field to a wide gap in the hedge, and turn left. There is a welcome bench here for resting. You will then emerge into a quiet tarmaced farm lane. Turn right, and continue down into **Mottisfont**.

6 Turn left through the village and left again down the road signposted for Broughton and Dunbridge. Watch out for a gap in the hedge after a few meters, signposted as a footpath by a fingerpost. Diagonally cross the arable field to the right, pass through the next wooded field boundary, and continue straight through the next arable field too. Dogs on leads well before the next field boundary. Pass around the gate, and turn right onto the road. keep well into the verge, and return to your car a few metres further up the road on the left hand side.

The buttercup meadow at point 4.

River Itchen and Shawford Down

The River Itchen.

This very pretty riverside loop beside the River Itchen is a great stroll for a morning or afternoon, and a rare spot of tranquil countryside between Winchester and Eastleigh. Take some time to relax and watch the river go by. Starting on top of Shawford Down, dogs can go off leads to release some energy, and there are lovely views over Shawford and Twyford. The walk then uses quiet residential roads through Shawford to the River Itchen, where dogs can go free again beside the peaceful river. The walk returns along the river to Shawford and back up Shawford Down. There are places along the river for a picnic and where water-loving dogs can have a swim or a paddle. The many rights of way in the area may encourage more adventurous souls to extend their walk – the Itchen Way runs for around 30 miles from Woolston in Southampton to Hinton Ampner!

Hampshire & the New Forest

Dog factors

Distance: 2½ miles.
Road walking: ¼ mile along a quiet village back road. The route crosses the main road through Shawford in two places.
Livestock: Possibility of cattle on Shawford Down, and in fields adjacent to the footpaths around Point 3.
Stiles: None.
Nearest vets: Stable Close Veterinary Clinic, Winchester (St Cross Road) or Chandlers Ford Veterinary Surgery, Chandlers Ford.

Terrain

A mostly very flat route along quiet village back roads and river paths, which can be narrow in places. Shawford Down presents a slightly more challenging element to the walk, with a hill to descend at the start and a steepish climb at the end, but you can take these at your own pace. If you prefer you could leave out the hill altogether and park at point 2.

Where to park

The free car park at the top of Shawford Down (GR: SU467248). Alternatively, there is parking in Shawford (SU473249), picking up the walk at point 2.
OS map: Explorer OL32 Winchester.

How to get there

Minutes from the M3, between Winchester and Eastleigh, the car park is accessed from a minor B road running between Chandlers Ford and Compton, which largely runs parallel to the M3. From the south, exit the M3 at junction 12 and follow signs for Otterbourne and Compton. The car park entrance comes up sharply on the right just before the right-hand turn for Shawford. From the north, exit at junction 11, turn right towards Winchester at the first roundabout and left at the next roundabout, nearly back on yourself, towards Compton and Otterbourne. The car park is on the left just after the turn for Shawford. Sat Nav: SO21 2BS

Nearest refreshments

The Bridge at Shawford is on the route, serves food and is dog- and walker-friendly (☎ 01962 713171). Further afield, the Bugle Inn at Twyford serves delicious locally-sourced food (☎ 01962 714888) and The Old Forge in Otterbourne is also worth a visit (☎ 01962 717191).

River Itchen and Shawford Down

The Walk

1 Pass through the kissing gate closest to the car park entrance into **Shawford Down**. Take the surfaced pathway diagonally to the left through the woodland, emerging into downland with pretty views across to Twyford. Keep on the footpath, going diagonally left, passing the **Shawford war memorial**, and aiming for Shawford at the bottom of the hill. Pass through the kissing gate. There is a further small car park at this point.

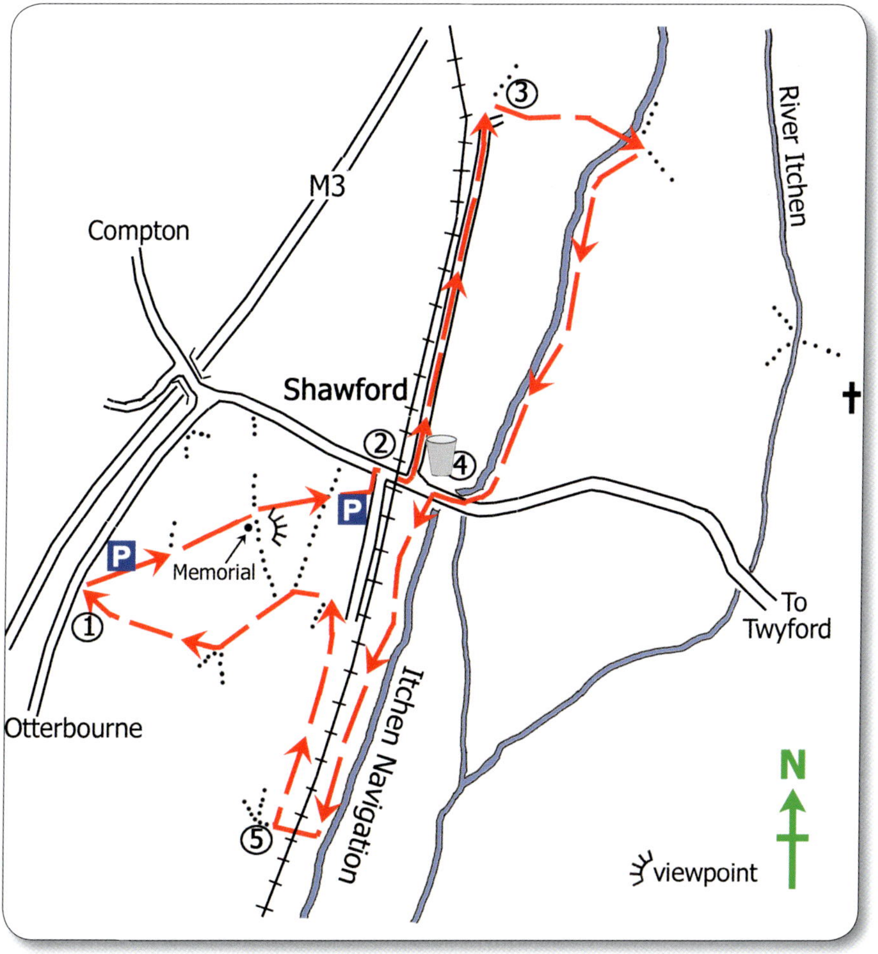

Hampshire & the New Forest

Shawford Down is a remnant of a much older medieval landscape of sheep-grazed hillsides, with water meadows in the river valleys, which existed in this area before arable farming took over as the more profitable business and the busy M3 corridor made its impact. The views over to the Twyford Downs, however, are still very beautiful.

❷ Turn left along the tarmac track, right onto the main Shawford to Twyford road and under the railway bridge. Cross over the road into **Bridge Lane,** passing between the **Bridge pub** and the railway line; this is a quiet residential access road with little traffic. Continue up a slight incline past the pub car park, passing houses to the right. *The London–Weymouth main line is down in a cutting to the left but there is sturdy fencing between your dog and the cutting.* The road goes downhill again. At the entrance to the driveway of **Kingsmere Meadows**, take the wooded footpath to the left of the drive and at the railway bridge turn right along the footpath.

❸ Continue over two streams on small footbridges and through a copse before reaching a narrow bridge crossing the **Itchen Navigation** (*with strong handrails for you but gaps at dog-height*) to the towpath. *If your dog loves swimming, there are some good spots slightly to the left.* You can also enjoy views over to historic Twyford, with the church clearly visible, and can cross the water meadows to the church and pubs here if you have time to explore. To continue the walk, turn right, enjoying scenes of the river and pretty gardens on the right-hand bank. Where the river divides, cross one channel on the wooden bridge, and continue up to the main road (*dogs on a lead here*).

The Itchen Navigation flows parallel to the River Itchen, and the channels join in places. The Navigation, however, is entirely man-made. Whilst the riverside scenes are tranquil and rural today, the waterway was constructed in the late 17th century to transport heavy industrial goods such as coal from ports at Southampton to Winchester. The various Itchen channels were also used to support water meadows and mills along its route. Occasional sluices and locks are still present today. The Navigation was eventually closed after competition from the railways made it redundant around 1850. Today, as well as a reminder of our industrial history, it is also a haven for wildlife.

❹ Cross over the main road, and take the path immediately to the left, between the river and houses. Continue along the river, and where the housing finishes, pass through the kissing gate into a meadow (**The Malms**). The path joins a tarmac track from the right and runs beside the river and the railway line up on a built embankment to the right. Continue along this path for 100 yards or so until you find an underpass to the right under the railway and enter **Shawford Down** via a kissing gate.

River Itchen and Shawford Down

5 There are numerous rights of way and permissive pathways through Shawford Down, which you could explore at your leisure. To return to your car, turn right, following the railway back on yourself on a wide woodland track. As the woodland opens out into grassland, turn left up the slope, and climb two steep flights of steps, emerging into a meadow. *There may be livestock at this point*. Follow the pathway diagonally to the left, then aim for the kissing gate you can see at the top of the field. Stop for breath and last views over Twyford, then pass through the kissing gate into the woodland and follow the woodland path back to point 1 and the car park.

Grazing the water meadows on the River Itchen.

8
New Alresford

The delightful Mill House.

Dogs can go off the lead for much of this walk along riverside paths and old drovers' routes through the fields of Abbotstone Down, with a possible swim in the river for the water-loving ones. The walk starts and ends in the very picturesque market town of New Alresford, where you can browse happily (if your dog companion/s allow) in the numerous tourist shops or find plenty of pubs and cafés. The route continues along the pretty River Alre, which joins the River Itchen just south of the walk. Both rivers are internationally important for biodiversity due to the clear chalk-fed waters, which are home to important plant and fish species. The clear waters are also ideal for watercress production. Alresford was once, and still is, the centre of watercress growing in Hampshire. In Victorian times, the old steam railway, now operating for visitors as far as Alton, transported the crop to London and beyond. The walk follows the Wayfarer's Walk out into the rolling chalk downland around the hamlet of Abbotstone, taking in views of the beautiful Itchen Valley, before returning to Alresford past more of the famous watercress beds.

New Alresford 8

Terrain
The route mostly uses good, well-trodden paths, well-surfaced gravel paths along the river and wide grassy or unsurfaced byways. The countryside around Alresford is pleasantly rolling, so expect some gentle climbs and steady ascents. Paths can be rutted in places, and may be muddy or slippery in winter.

Where to park
Parking along Broad Street is limited to 2 hours only, so it is best to use the longer stay pay and display car park at the Watercress Line steam railway. This is well signposted, just off the B3047 in the centre of the town (GR: SU588325). **OS map:** Explorer OL32 Winchester.

How to get there
New Alresford is located between Winchester and Alton, and signposted from the A31. Whether arriving from the east or west, you will come in on the B3047, which passes the top end of Broad Street through the centre of the town. Follow signs to the Watercress Line off the B3047 onto Station Road. Sat Nav: SO24 9JG

Nearest refreshments
There are a good choice of pubs, cafes and restaurants in and around Alresford. The Bell, The Horse and Groom, and The Globe all serve food and are dog friendly. Further afield, the Bush Inn at Ovington (off the B3047) is

Dog factors
Distance: 4½ miles.
Road walking: On pavements through New Alresford, and a few hundred yards on quiet rural lanes at Abbotstone. The walk is intersected in a couple of places by rural roads that you will need to cross.
Livestock: Other than swans on the river, there is the possibility of cattle in occasional fields between points 3 and 4 and through Abbotstone, although the drove routes pass between fields not through them. There could be cattle in one field between 5 and 6.
Stiles: 1 stile and 2 gates between points 5 and 6. The stile is passable by most small and medium breeds of dog, in gaps underneath.
Nearest vets: Cedar Veterinary Group, New Alresford.

Hampshire & the New Forest

also worth a visit. This riverside pub is dog-friendly and serves great food, but it's very popular so book in advance.

The Walk

1. Exit the car park via **Station Road**, heading back towards the centre of New Alresford. Turn right into **West Street**, cross over the road and turn left down **Broad Street**, enjoying the attractive buildings and shops as you pass. *As an alternative, you can turn right into the pretty churchyard from Station Road, left through the churchyard and exit opposite Broad Street.* Where the road forks, take the left-hand fork (**Mill Hill**) then turn left into **Ladywell Lane**, following signs for the **Wayfarer's Walk**. Continue down the lane to the river and carry straight on along the riverside path to the very picturesque **Mill House** cottage.

2. Ignoring the pathway to the right in front of the cottage carry on along the river. When the path emerges onto a residential road, turn right in front of the houses (still following **Wayfarer's Walk** signs) and continue along the river. Eventually the footpath crosses the river into a copse. Ignore the stile

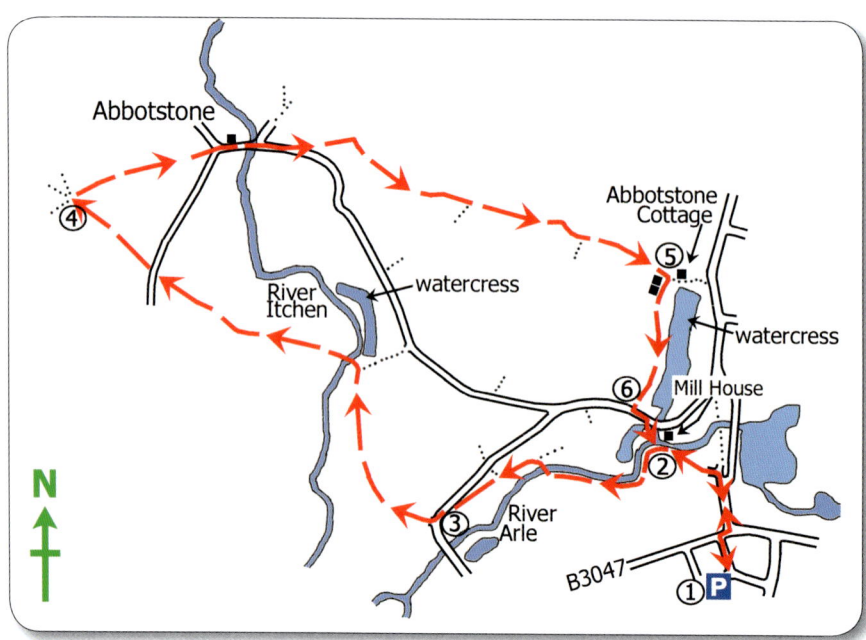

New Alresford

and footpath to the right; turn left and follow the path up a slight ascent. Pass in front of the houses (following the 'private drive/footpath' sign) and out between the fields, keeping to the field boundary on the left.

❸ On joining a rural road, take the drove road to the right, still signposted **Wayfarer's Walk**. Continue along this byway for ½ mile or so. At the T-junction of byways take the left-hand fork, past a watercress farm on the right-hand side. Pass to the left of the farm, and continue straight on along the byway, enjoying occasional views of the Alre valley to the right. The byway narrows to a footpath, then comes out onto a rural road. Cross over the road and continue along the byway until you come to a meeting of paths.

❹ Take the right-hand path – a grassy byway leading downhill. This eventually emerges into the hamlet of **Abbotstone**. Ignoring the rural roads to the right and left, cross over the road and continue straight on, passing some picturesque cottages on the left, and fields to the right. When the road forks in a dip, continue straight on up the hill and then take the pathway to the left-hand side. This bends to the right slightly, then continue straight on along this pathway for a mile or so, ignoring two footpaths to the right.

❺ On sight of **Abbotstone Cottage** on the left, turn right down a driveway (signposted 'footpath') and pass a few large houses. Take the footpath straight on between a large brick house on the right and a barn. Following the footpath signs, pass through a stile (with a gate to the side) up into the fields. Keeping the field boundary and views of watercress beds to the left, negotiate another stile, then a gate, emerging onto a long driveway past the watercress beds.

❻ At the end of the driveway turn left onto the lane, and then go right into a byway just before the road crosses a stream. You will soon recognise the **Mill House** passed at point 2. Retrace your steps through **New Alresford** back to your car.

Grazing in the watermeadows at Abbotstone.

Old Winchester Hill

The splendid chalk downland at point 2 of the route.

In the heart of the South Downs National Park, Old Winchester Hill is beautiful in any season, uplifting in winter and a great place to soak up summer sunshine, and has fine views over the very English chalk hills. Dogs can go off the lead along the railway line and will enjoy rural smells and a good stretch of the legs. The starting point is a walk round to the tip of Old Winchester Hill, an Iron Age hill fort and National Nature Reserve (NNR), down the hill onto an old railway line in the lovely Meon Valley, and returning on rural lanes and through farmland back up the hill. A steepish ascent and incline, together with the distance, makes this one of the more challenging routes in the book, but it is well worth it. At 197 m (646 ft) Old Winchester Hill is amongst Hampshire's highest, although it misses out on the accolade of being a Marilyn (the Munros' shorter siblings) as it is a few metres short of the required 150 m (492 ft) relative drop in height.

Terrain

Well-used national footpaths, mainly on farmland, rural lanes, and a flat and well-surfaced old railway line, where you are likely to encounter cyslists. Paths down from the hill can be a little muddy or slippery in winter, but generally well maintained. An easy walk to navigate, with well-signposted paths, and Old Winchester Hill being visible in most places as a landmark.

Old Winchester Hill (9)

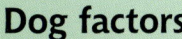

Dog factors
Distance: 6 miles.
Road walking: 1 mile along very quiet rural lanes.
Livestock: Sheep in adjacent fields.
Stiles: 1.
Nearest vets: Shield Veterinary Centre, Bishops Waltham, or St Peters Veterinary Group, Petersfield.

Where to park
Old Winchester Hill National Nature Reserve free car park (GR: SU645214).
OS map: Explorer OL3 Meon Valley.

How to get there
Old Winchester Hill lies between Meonstoke and East Meon. The car park is best accessed from the A32, signposted from Warnford. It is possible to come cross-country from the A3 to Clanfield or East Meon and up onto the downs from there. Sat Nav: GU32 1HW

Nearest refreshments
The Buck's Head in Meonstoke lies within 200 yards of the toures, serves food, has a beer garden and is dog-and walker-friendly. ☎ 01489 877313. There are also several lovely dog friendly pubs which serve food within a short drive including the George and Falcon at Warnford ☎ 07958 124285, Thomas Lord at West Meon ☎ 01730 829244, The Shoe at Exton ☎ 01489 877526, and the Bat and Ball, Hambledon ☎ 02392 632692

The Walk

1 Go through the kissing gate opposite the road entrance into **Old Winchester Hill National Nature Reserve**. Turn left and start along the path leading to the hill fort. This bends round to the right, with stunning views over the hill fort and surrounding South Downs.
   The summit of the hill is an Iron Age hill fort, but there are earlier Bronze Age barrows within the hill fort itself dating from between 4,500 and 3,500 BC.

2 At the hill fort itself ignore signs for the **South Downs Way** to the left and enter the hill fort via the gate. After exploring the site and enjoying the views, take the path leading straight over the hill fort, past a trig point and

Hampshire & the New Forest

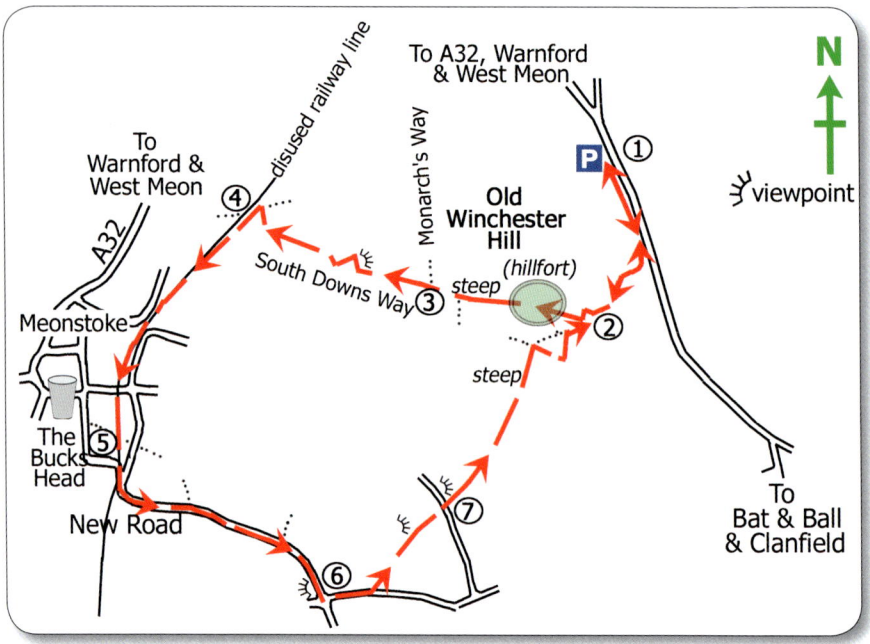

view-marker, and down the slope straight ahead. Exit the NNR and continue downhill.

The chalk downlands are likely to have been farmed since Neolithic times, so this is a truly ancient landscape. The chalk grassland is nationally important for wildlife including numerous butterfly species and orchids.

❸ At a fork in the path take the **South Downs Way** path signposted straight on (round the gap in the hedge). Ignore signs for the **Monarch's Way** to the right. Continue straight down the hill, past fields of sheep and taking in a few zigzags, until you get to the bottom.

❹ The path crosses over a dry stream via a bridge. Turn left and go up the slight incline ahead to the railway line. Turn left onto the old line, and continue along it for just over a mile – crossing one road and going under a railway bridge.

The Meon Valley Railway was built in 1898 and ran from London to Fareham and Gosport via Alton, East Tisted, Droxford and Wickham. It closed in 1955, long before the Beeching Report, due to unsustainable passenger numbers. The old railway line is now part of the Meon Valley Trail which links Wickham and West Meon.

Old Winchester Hill

5 On the approach to a second railway bridge, just after a little bridge crossing a footpath below, look out for a broad path off the railway line to the right. Exit onto a rural road and, taking care with dogs on the road, turn left, left again over the railway line, then at a T-junction take the right-hand road, **New Road**. Follow this road round to the left, and continue up the hill, taking your time as it is quite steep for Hampshire. *This is a very quiet rural lane, but you will encounter occasional cars and farm traffic, so do use your own judgement in relation to whether your dog goes on the lead.*

6 At a junction in the road turn left, and soon after look out for fingerpost signs for the **Wayfarer's Walk** on the left next to a metal farm gate. Go through the gap in the hedge (there is a stile but no fence so dogs and people can pass through easily) and walk downhill, keeping to the field boundary. At the end of a second field pass over a stile on the right and continue straight on to exit the field onto a rural farm road. Pause to enjoy the views straight ahead of **Old Winchester Hill**, and the classic farmed English landscape of the South Downs.

7 Continue down the farm driveway straight ahead (**Stocks Down Farm**). Pass the farmhouse and continue straight on along the field boundary, where the path starts to climb. At the top of the field, and a junction of paths, pick up the **South Downs Way**. This path leads through a gap in the hedge to the right of the gate back into the NNR, and straight up the hill. The path takes a right-hand turn and comes out at the entrance to the NNR at point 2. Turn right to retrace your steps.

View back to Old Winchester Hill from the Meon Valley Trail.

Hawkley's Hangers

Looking over the scarp of Ashford Hanger.

This truly beautiful area of the South Downs National Park is known as 'Little Switzerland', a landscape of woodlands, sunken lanes and drove roads, steep hills and mixed farmland. The wooded slopes are known as hangers, from the ancient English 'hangra'. Although not the longest route in the book, it is one of the more challenging due to the steep slopes. Dogs can go off the lead for much of the walk, and you will all sleep soundly after those hills!

The ancient hanger woodlands of beech and yew are internationally important woodlands for their biodiversity interest, and this landscape is associated with the naturalist Gilbert White who lived in nearby Selborne and studied the plants and animals of the hangers. The First World War poet Edward Thomas also lived in nearby Steep for a time before he was killed in battle in 1917, and extensively walked in these hills, which inspired some of his finest work, contrasting the peace and quiet found here with the horrors of the battlefield.

The walk initially follows the Hangers Way through pretty meadows and woodlands, then goes up into the wooded hangers on old drove roads, emerging onto a ridgeway from where there are two dramatic viewpoints

Hawkley's Hangers 10

looking south and then north; well worth the climb and a chance to catch your breath before descending back down the hanger to Hawkley, where a welcoming dog- and walker-friendly village pub awaits. The pretty Victorian village church with its unusual tower is also well worth a visit.

Terrain
Easy to follow, on well-trodden and well-marked footpaths, rural lanes and old drovers' byways. Challenging steep slopes up and down the hangers, so well worth bringing poles if you use them, and these steep chalk paths can be rutted and slippery in winter.

Where to park
On-street parking in the village so do be considerate to residents. The village green (GR: SU745291) and roadside opposite the pub (SU747291) are the two best spots. **OS map:** Explorer OL33 Haslemere & Petersfield.

How to get there
Hawkley is 2 miles or so from the A3, and also signposted from the A32. Exit the A3 at the turn-off for Liss and Selborne, taking the B3006 towards Liss. The road for Hawkley and the Hawkley Inn are signposted from West Liss, leading you back over the A3. After a mile or so watch out for the signs for the village and pub to the left. Sat Nav: GU33 6NE

Nearest refreshments
The viewpoints at 4A and 4B on the sketch map are great picnic or coffee spots, so take your refreshments with you as there are no cafés or pubs on the way round. The Hawkley Inn is, however, well worth a visit on your return, serving food and a great selection of well-kept ales and other refreshments,

Dog factors
Distance: 4 miles.
Road walking: Almost a mile in total, but using quiet sunken lanes with very little through-traffic.
Livestock: None usually but there is the possibility of encountering cattle between points 1 and 2 in the meadow areas.
Stiles: 2 between points 1 and 2, one very dog-friendly, and the second fine for smaller and more agile breeds.
Nearest vets: Liss Veterinary Surgery (St Peter's Vets).

Hampshire & the New Forest

and is dog-friendly to boot with stone floors inside the bar area, rustic benches at the front to watch the world going past (nice and slowly) or a large beer garden out the back. Website: www.hawkleyinn.co.uk; ☎ 01730 827205.

The Walk

❶ From the top of the triangular village green (with the church and post box behind you) proceed down **Cheesecombe Farm Lane**, signposted '**Hangers Way**' towards Queen Elizabeth Country Park. As the lane dips down, move onto the driveway on the right, then on the bend turn off left onto the Hangers Way footpath. This dips down into a pretty meadow. Ignore the footpath straight on and follow the Hangers Way signs diagonally across the field. Stay on this footpath for another ½ mile, through meadows and woodland

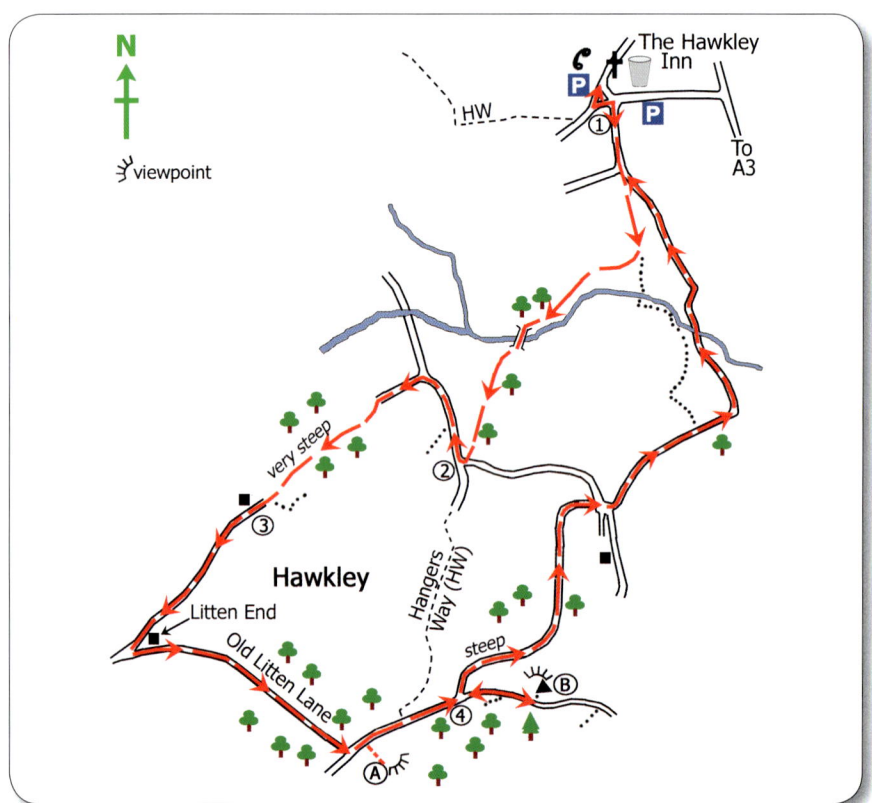

Hawkley's Hangers

edge, across **Oakshott Stream**, and across stile 1. The path bends to the left to eventually emerge onto a rural road at **Middle Oakshott Farm**, crossing stile 2.

Dogs will need to stay under control across the farmland. There is the possibility of encountering cattle on this part of the route, particularly in the winter months. Stile 1 is reasonably low and sturdy so some dogs will be able to cross it. There is also a dog-hole in the fence to the right which smaller breeds will be able to use. Stile 2 is less sturdy but there is a gap under the fence to the left, which the more agile breeds will be able to use. Our pointer had no problems with either.

2 Leaving the **Hangers Way** here (which is a shorter route but has several further stiles, many of them not suitable for dogs), turn right down the lane, and continue for 300 yards or so. Ignore the first footpath sign on the left, and look out for a bridleway sign. Turn left into the field and pass around the earth mounds to the bridleway, which runs beside the field boundary. Dogs can go off the leads along the bridleway. The bridleway soon starts to ascend, passing a small orchard and deserted farm buildings before ascending sharply up **Happersnapper Hanger**. *Do take your time climbing the hanger as it is extremely steep and may be slippery in winter!*

3 At the top of the hanger you will emerge onto a rural lane, passing a couple of properties. Continue along the road to **Litten End**, and go left onto **Old Litten Lane**. This eventually turns into an unsurfaced byway. At the T-junction turn left, continuing down Old Litten Lane.

You are now at the top of a ridge with steep drops to the right and left. It is well worth taking some time to explore and have a drink-stop or picnic at one of the two viewpoints marked A and B on the sketch map.

Viewpoint A is 50 yards or so to the right along the Hangers Way path – a superb viewpoint over the scarp of Ashford Hanger to the hills of the South Downs beyond. Viewpoint B is 150 yards further on down Old Litten Lane beyond point 4, taking the set of steps on the left up to a trig point and further great views over the ridge. Retrace your steps.

4 If you aren't stopping to look at the views, continue past waymarkers for the Hangers Way to the right and the left, to a T-junction with a byway to the left. Turn left onto this byway (right if coming from Viewpoint B) and proceed with some caution down the steep wooded slope. After ¼ mile or so you will emerge onto a narrow rural lane. Turn right onto the lane, and almost immediately left back onto the unsurfaced byway. Continue along this track for another ¼ mile, until it eventually becomes a surfaced lane. Carry on up the hill into **Hawkley**. The **Hawkley Inn** is a short distance to the right for a very welcome drink!

Ludshott Common and Grayshott

On Ludshott Common.

A lovely circular walk taking in a variety of scenery, including ponds, heathlands and woodlands around Grayshott, with views across to the South Downs, and better still, no stiles at all. Dogs can roam free in the woodland areas along much of the route, and there are three big ponds to swim in at the start or end of the walk. This picturesque and well-wooded part of the East Hampshire Weald is often forgotten in favour of the South Downs or Devil's Punchbowl across the border but offers some great walking. Undulating in nature it takes in several short hills and heathland terrain so is challenging in places, although those preferring a short stroll could do a 1-mile loop to explore Waggoners Wells from where the walk begins.

Ludshott Common and Grayshott 11

Terrain
A steep climb and ascent, and rough terrain on the heath. The walk is mainly on woodland paths (often on wide tracks but some rougher paths) and sandy heathland tracks. The abundance of small heathland paths can make the route difficult to interpret in places so an OS map is a must. Some stretches are likely to be muddy in rainy weather and winter. Dogs need to be kept under close control in the heathland areas at nesting time.

Where to park
The National Trust free car park at the Waggoners Wells (GR: SU863344). There is an alternative free car park, also National Trust, ½ mile further up the road at Ludshott Common (SU853358), picking up the longer walk at point 6. **OS map:** Explorer OL33 Haslemere & Petersfield.

How to get there
Grayshott is near Haslemere just off the A3 in north east Hampshire. The village is signposted from the A3 and Waggoners Wells is also signposted from the roundabout. The route from the A3 brings you through the village on the B3002; follow this road straight on towards Headley. On the outskirts of the village, some ¾ mile from the centre, look out for Waggoners Wells Lane on the left, on a bend,(currently only signposted from the other direction). The car park is ½ mile down this lane. Sat Nav: GU26 6DT

Nearest refreshments
Dogs are welcome at The Fox and Pelican in Grayshott with treats on arrival. For their owners, food is freshly cooked and locally sourced. There is a large beer garden (☎ 01428 604757); www.foxandpelican.co.uk.

Dog factors
Distance: 1 mile or 4½ miles.
Road walking: None.
Livestock: Possibility of encountering cattle on Ludshott Common, particularly in the autumn and winter months; they graze the common and help to keep the scrub down.
Stiles: None
Nearest vets: Amery Vets, Grayshott.

Hampshire & the New Forest

The Walk

1 Take the steps at the far end of the car park and descend to the large pond in front of you. Turn left in front of the pond and follow the path. This goes down past a man-made water channel to two more large ponds.

Dogs can enjoy a good swim in the ponds or can stretch their legs in the woodlands well away from any cars! The Waggoners Well ponds are man-made, thought to date from at least the 17th century and possibly built as part of the Wealden iron smelting industry. They were later used as fish ponds, and are now managed by the National Trust.

Take the woodland path to the left, which ascends slightly away from the ponds, initially following a small stream down to the right. After 150 yards or so take the right-hand fork and continue along this woodland path until it descends to a meeting of paths and a bridge crossing the stream. Take care going down to the bridge.

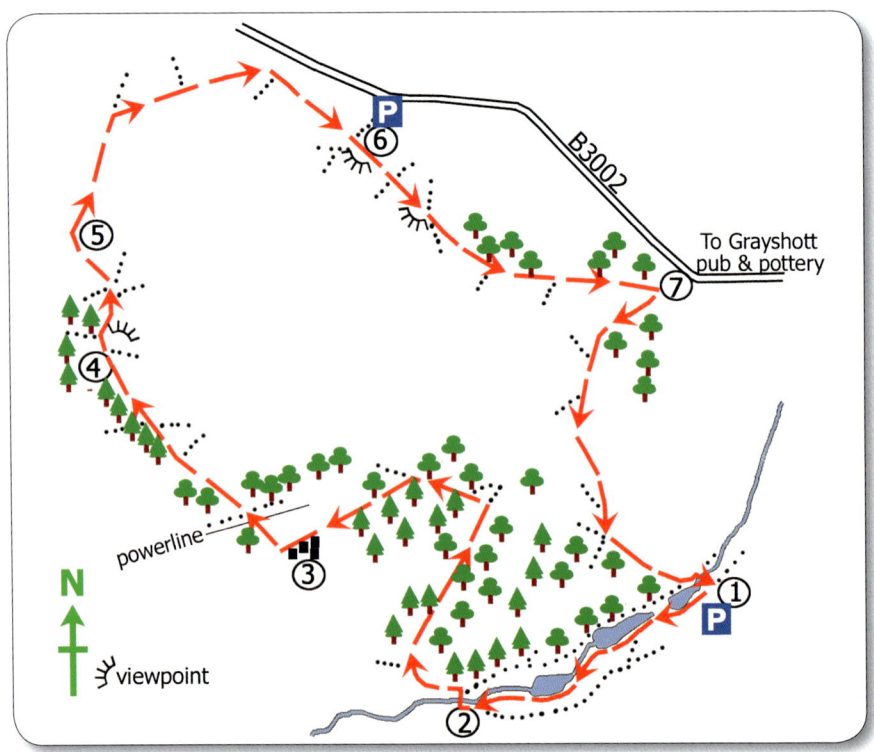

Ludshott Common and Grayshott ⑪

② Cross the stream. *Those wanting a short stroll can return to the car here by turning right and looping back on the other side of the ponds.* Otherwise, turn left along the bridleway, which goes uphill through the woodland – the first of the steady climbs of the walk. Ignore the stile and footpath to the left. After ½ mile or so from the ponds the path forks. Take the left-hand fork, marked as a bridleway with a small blue marker. You will then exit onto a wide woodland track. Turn left along this bridleway, and after a few hundred yards keep to the left as the path bends round. You then come to a few isolated houses set into the woodland.

③ Continue straight on past the houses back into the woodland, and just beyond the houses you will come to a crossing of woodland paths. Turn right here and continue forward, emerging after a few minutes onto a wide woodland track with a powerline overhead. Pass over this track and continue straight on. After a few minutes more the path is joined by a wide sandy track as you emerge onto a more open area of scrub. Keep going straight on along this new track, into a slight dip and rise to an open heathland area (ignore a small track to the right, and a crossing of paths in the dip).

The National Trust requests that dogs be kept under close control in the heathland area in spring and summer months due to ground nesting birds. This means keeping them to the main paths, which can be tricky for energetic dogs who like to run – although there are plenty of smells to keep more sedate dogs on the main paths anyway!

④ On reaching the second crossing of wide paths, pause for breath and enjoy the views over **Ludshott Common** from the handy bench. Ignore the wide bridleway to the right and left and take the smaller woodland path straight ahead. Take the right-hand fork and continue downhill to the bottom of the dip and a meeting of several woodland paths – ignore a small path on the right and the larger path to the right, instead following the path round to the left, and almost immediately taking the next right-hand fork. This takes you uphill and out onto open heathland.

⑤ At the top of the hill turn right onto a wide sandy track and continue straight on, enjoying views back across the heathland to the distant South Downs. After ¼ mile or so, the track passes close to housing on the left and bends round to the right (ignore the grassy path straight ahead here). Continue along this wide heathland track for a further ½ mile or so, passing through occasional patches of birch woodland until you spot **Ludshott Common car park** to the left, with further bench opportunites (and a dog poo bin).

⑥ Continue along the sandy track for a further ¼ mile or so to a distinct fork. We leave the wide sandy track here, which bends sharply round to the right into

Hampshire & the New Forest

the open heathland whilst we follow the more wooded path straight ahead, following the site boundary on the left. After a hundred yards or so, the new path also bends off to the right. Once more take the narrower wooded path straight on, with occasional views of Grayshott Hall through the trees to the left. Just over ¼ mile further on (ignoring any paths to the right) you will emerge onto a concrete path. (*Take care with wide-roaming dogs here, as the main road is not far away and is accessible to the left. The concrete path is a vehicle access path so there may be very occasional vehicles at this point too. The concrete standings in the area are relics from the First World War and the Second World War, one of four Canadian army camps attached to Bramshott Military Camp*).

7 Turn right along the concrete track, continuing through the woodland until the track widens. The main route bends round to the right but here continue straight on past vehicle barriers, still on concrete. After 50 yards or so, the concrete stops, and the woodland path continues, bending slightly to the left. After a set of telegraph poles, the path is joined by another woodland path from the left. Follow this path to the right. After 100 yards or so at a distinct crossroads of paths, turn left. The track soon dips steeply downhill, emerging onto Waggoner's Wells Lane at the edge of the ponds. Turn right and over the ford back to your car.

Strolling near Waggoners Wells.

North Hayling

Northney Farm near point 5 of the walk.

This part of Hayling feels more like East Anglia than Hampshire, with wide flat fields and rewarding views over the wide marshes and mudflats of the Langstone and Chichester harbours. Here numerous sailing boats test out the wind in the harbour waters, and views over the marinas are set off by the hills of the South Downs in the distance. Dogs can go off leads on most of the rights of way, and will enjoy the sea scents arriving on the breeze. The trail uses footpaths through the fields into the village of North Hayling, past the 12th-century church, St Peter's, and out to Northney Marshes and a viewpoint along the coastline before returning into the village. The coastline here is part of the Chichester Harbour Area of Outstanding Natural Beauty, and is also internationally important for wildlife, especially birds, so do bring the binoculars. This less well-known part of Hayling Island avoids the crowds heading south to the beach in sunny weather, but you could make a day of

Hampshire & the New Forest

> **Dog factors**
>
> **Distance:** 4 miles
> **Road walking:** A few yards on a B road to get to and from the car park, plus a road crossing and a few hundred yards on village roads in Northney. The route also crosses through a quiet residential estate between points 6 and 7.
> **Livestock:** Cattle after point 2 and horse paddocks around point 7.
> **Stiles:** 3, all with good dog-gaps underneath, but there is a stile-free return option for those wishing to avoid them.
> **Nearest vets:** Harbour Veterinary Group, or Vets4Pets, both Hayling Island.

it with fish and chips on the seafront. Most of the beaches are dog-friendly, although there are restrictions in some places in the summer months.

Terrain

An entirely flat walk in a figure-of-eight loop, using rights of way through farmland, permissive paths on Northney Common, and small sections on village roads. All footpaths are in good condition. The permissive paths are not waymarked, but the flat landscape makes it easy to navigate and you can always see where you are in relation to the coast.

Where to park

The free car park at the entrance to North Common (GR: SU727038).
OS map: Explorer OL8 Chichester.

How to get there

From the A27 to the east of Portsmouth, take the exit signposted for Hayling Island and Langstone, and follow signs for the A3023 onto Hayling. Just after the bridge onto the island take the first road on the left, signposted to Northney and the Langstone Hotel. The car park is on the left-hand side just after the first welcome signs for Northney. Sat Nav: PO11 0ND

Nearest refreshments

The Northney Farm Tea Rooms ☎ 02392 467607 are located 400 yards from the start of the walk in Northney village. The Salt Shack Café is within a few minutes' drive in Northney Marina (☎ 02392 468843). The Ship Inn (☎ 02392 471719) and the Royal Oak (☎ 02392 483125) are the closest pubs across the harbour in Langstone. All cafés and pubs are dog-friendly.

North Hayling 12

The Walk

1 With dogs on leads initially, exit onto the road and turn right onto **Northney Road**, staying on the pavement. You will shortly see a footpath sign on the other side of the road, running to the side of the recreation ground; cross over and turn left down this path. This emerges into a large arable field on the right. *Dogs need to be under control through this farmland but there is no livestock.* Following the field boundary, the path turns sharp left and then right round the field corners, and starts to skirt round the backs of houses in **Northney**. On reaching a kissing gate at the next corner of the field, exit the field into the churchyard.

Northney and the surrounding villages have a rich history; they were once part of Saxon Hayling Manor, owned by the Crown and the monks of St Swithuns, Winchester, until given to the Abbey of Jumièges, Normandy by William the Conqueror. St Peter's church dates from 1140, and was built by the Jumièges monks. A chancel and north chapel were added in 1250. There are a few shady benches in the churchyard if you need a rest.

2 Turn left towards the church, and put dogs on a lead temporarily whilst you exit onto **St Peters Road** and cross over into **Church Lane** directly opposite, a quiet residential access road. The road zigzags right, then left, around a couple of quaint thatched cottages, and then starts to turn into a farm track. A gap to the side of the gate takes you onto **Northney Common** and the section of the route on permissive pathways.

The permissive paths through Northney Common are on private land, which is open to the public by the landowner's permission, so please note they may be subject to cancellation or change. The route is a popular one with local dog walkers, so you will be in good company, but please do make sure your dog is under close control. There are cattle in some of the fields. Northney Farm runs a shop from Stoke, where you can buy local produce, including Three Harbours Beef and Northney ice-cream.

3 Continue along the track until you come to three metal farm gates. Take the smaller wooden gate to the right and follow the pathway fenced off between fields. The path curves round to the left and then opens out onto the coastline. Go across the short 1.5 m (5 ft) ditch (this is bridged by large railway sleepers – substantial but with no hand rails), and up a few steps onto the sea wall. Turn right along a short section of coastline.

Do stop to look at the coastal views across Chichester Harbour to Thorney Island. The coastline and harbour are part of the Chichester Harbour Area of Outstanding Natural Beauty.

Hampshire & the New Forest

④ At the next fenceline turn right down the steps and across the ditch (similar bridge as before) back down into the fields. Follow the pathway straight ahead, walking towards a tall row of evergreen trees. Turn right in front of the trees, following the field boundary, and halfway along pass left through the gap in the trees onto a shingle path. Turn right, onto a tarmaced residential road, then left (**St Peters Avenue**), and follow this back to **St Peters Road**. You can avoid walking along too much of the road by crossing over to the village hall and phonebox on the right, and turning left down the narrow footpath to the side of the hall (signed with a fingerpost). Turn right into the arable field, again skirting the backs of Northney houses; after 50 yards or so you will come to a crossroads of footpaths.

⑤ *At this point you can return to the car, avoiding stiles, by taking the path straight ahead and through a kissing gate into the churchyard, and retracing your steps, which will lead you to the start of point 2.* For the full walk, turn left along the broad farm track (a short distance in front of the churchyard) through arable fields, marked with yellow footpath symbols. This turns left again, following a field corner and then diagonally right through the fields. At a crossroads of footpaths ignore the path joining from the left and continue

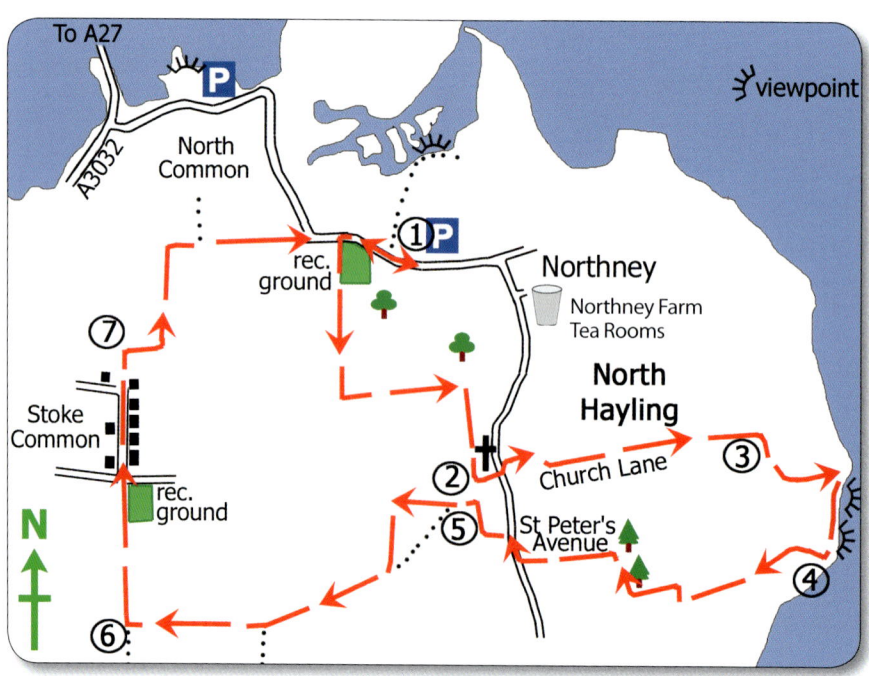

North Hayling 12

straight on, keeping fields to your right and a ditch and hedgerow trees to the left. At the end of the field cross over stile 1 (*a two-bar fence with good dog-gaps around (17–19 ins) high underneath, restricting only the tallest, widest or less agile dogs*). Continue straight on and cross stile 2 (similar to stile 1).

6 Turn right onto a concrete track. Go past the waterworks building and straight on between a hedgerow and fence, emerging into quiet residential roads of **Stoke Common**. Cross over and continue straight along the road ahead (**Kingsway**) through the estate, cross over again, and follow the footpath straight ahead between the houses into the fields behind (horses may be present here, but there is good fencing all the way along the path).

7 Follow the path as it zigzags to the right and left, then go through the gap in the hedge to join another footpath. Turn right and cross stile 3 (similar again to stile 1). Continue along the field edge until the footpath turns into a driveway. Dogs on leads here as you go past the house and straight onto **Northney Road**. There is no pavement for a few yards but a wide verge. Continue straight on until you reach the car park.

St Peter's church in North Hayling.

Titchfield to the Solent

The Solent coastline at point 4 of the walk.

Dogs can go off the lead for much of this flat rectangular walk to the Solent and back, and there are some fine sea views, picnic spots and dog-swimming areas along the coastline. Starting in the historic village of Titchfield, the route uses wide farm tracks across the flat coastal plain to get down to the Solent, where it joins the Solent Way. There are views across to the New Forest and to the Isle of Wight, plenty of boats in the Solent to watch, and dogs can swim in the sea. The walk then returns on low clifftops and flat footpaths alongside the Titchfield Canal.

Terrain
Easy to navigate and very flat with a gentle climb onto shallow cliffs on the coastline. Uses well-marked footpaths, farm tracks and surfaced paths. A short distance through Titchfield on quiet residential roads, with two short stretches along busier B roads. Coastal stretches and the upper unsurfaced canal path can be muddy after rain.

Titchfield to the Solent 13

Where to park
The Titchfield Canal free car park off Bridge Street, Titchfield (GR: SU542055).
OS map: Explorer OL3 Meon Valley.

How to get there
Titchfield is located between Fareham and Locks Heath, just off the A27 and a short drive from the M27. From the A27 follow signs to Titchfield Village. You will either come in from the west via Southampton Hill (at the end turn right into High Street) or from the east via Titchfield Hill (follow this road round into East Street then High Street). From High Street continue straight on into South Street, and take the left exit at the mini roundabout onto Bridge Street. The car park is on the right just by the traffic-calming system. Keep your eyes peeled for the footpath sign, which runs past the car park along the canal. Sat Nav: PO14 4EA

Nearest refreshments
There are several pubs in Titchfield. The Bugle Hotel (☎ 01329 846393), The Queens Head (☎ 01329 842154), and the Wheatsheaf (☎ 01329 842965). Titchfield Mill (tel 01329 840931) and the Fishermans Rest (tel 01329 845065) are also close by. All serve food and are dog friendly.

The Walk

1 Starting off with dogs on leads, turn right from the car park into **Bridge Street**, cross onto the pavement and walk left towards the village. At the mini-roundabout, turn left onto **Coach Hill**, and walk up the slight incline. Take the

Dog factors
Distance: 5½ miles.
Road walking: 1/3 mile on residential roads, 50 yds or so along a busier B road.
Livestock: Possibility of horses in fields around Titchfield.
Stiles: 2, both with good dog-gaps, and one can be avoided via a short diversion.
Nearest vets: Companion Care in Fareham or the Alver Veterinary Group in Stubbington and Fareham.

Hampshire & the New Forest

second residential road on the left, **Lower Bellfield**. Continue straight on to the end of the road.

② Pass through the short alley between the housing, past a row of garages and then into the field ahead. There is a fixed barrier here at waist height, which you will need to go under or over, but which presents no obstacles for dogs. *Dogs can go off lead here to let off some steam, and it is a good field for ball throwing etc. Cross the field diagonally, heading for the far right corner, but do note that dogs will need to go back on leads well before the end of the field, as they can easily get onto the busy B road beyond.* Cross over stile 1 and turn left into this road (**Posbrook Lane**).

Stile 1 has good gaps of around 15 ins underneath, which all but tall non-agile breeds will be able to get under. Our two labradors managed this with no difficulty. If you need to avoid this stile, however, at the end of point 1, turn right into **Bellfield** *before the alleyway. Continue to the end of the road, then turn left into* **Posbrook Lane**, *and follow this road along to meet up with the field and stile 1 at the end of it. There is a road verge but no pavement, so do keep well in as cars can be fast along here despite the 30 mph zone.*

③ Continue along the road on the verge for 50 yards, then turn right into a driveway and footpath, marked with a fingerpost and adverts for a camping and caravan site. Go through the kissing gate and continue along the drive until the crossing of paths in front of a large property to the right. Take the left-hand fork, following the hedgerow and out into arable fields. *Dogs should be under close control across this farmland, and there may be horses in the first field.*

④ Follow this track straight on between the fields for just over a mile towards the coast. The track becomes surfaced after **Brownwich Lane**, and you will pass a few farms and houses. When you reach the coast avoid the driveway of **Sea Houses** to the left, taking the track to the right, which emerges onto the shoreline.

⑤ Turn left in front of the large pond, and follow the **Solent Way** up the slight incline onto the soft cliffs.

Water-loving dogs will love the pond ahead; ours raced through, having a great time. You can also get to the beach for picnics, resting, beachcombing and swimming on calm sunny days – both you and your dog! Don't get caught by the tides though if you do take a wander along the beach as the high watermark can come right up to the cliffs. There are also a few bench spots with great views on the cliffs above.

Follow the pathway along the clifftops. Ignore the pathway to the left, inland, after ½ mile or so. The coast path also splits into two forks here, but they reconnect later on. There can be muddy stretches here. The pathway

Titchfield to the Solent 13

eventually narrows, passing in front of a large fenceline at **Cliff Cottages**, and starts going down a slight slope – at the bottom of the hill pass through a gate and through the **Meon Shore Chalets** to the road. *Dogs on a lead here as the road beyond can be busy with visitors.*

6 If you want a refreshment stop at this point, you can continue along the road (use the seafront path to avoid the road) to the café at **Titchfield Haven**. If not, cross over and pass through the kissing gate on the left into a meadow (part of Titchfield Haven), and follow the signposted right of way to the left.

Titchfield Haven is a nature reserve, particularly important for wintering birds, located on the lower reaches of the River Meon, with reedbed, marsh and fen habitats. The main part of the reserve is accessed via a second gate near the visitor centre, but there is an entry fee and dogs are not allowed in. It is still worth taking your binoculars as you can usually see plenty of birds from the road, and wading birds and wildfowl along the shoreline and in the reserve. You can see into the water meadows at various points along the route.

Continue straight along this path back inland for 2 miles, first around the fields and marshes, then entering woodland, and emerging into farmland, and always following the boundary of **Titchfield Haven** to the right. *Dogs can go off leads all the way along, but do note that the road is adjacent to the left for a few hundred yards, and can be accessed by exploring dogs in a few places. Stile 2 comes after ¼ mile or so but has a proper gap for dogs to the left of the gate.* The path eventually becomes surfaced; you will find the car park on the right-hand side. For anyone wishing to explore **Titchfield** by foot, the canal path continues up to **St Peter's church** and the village.

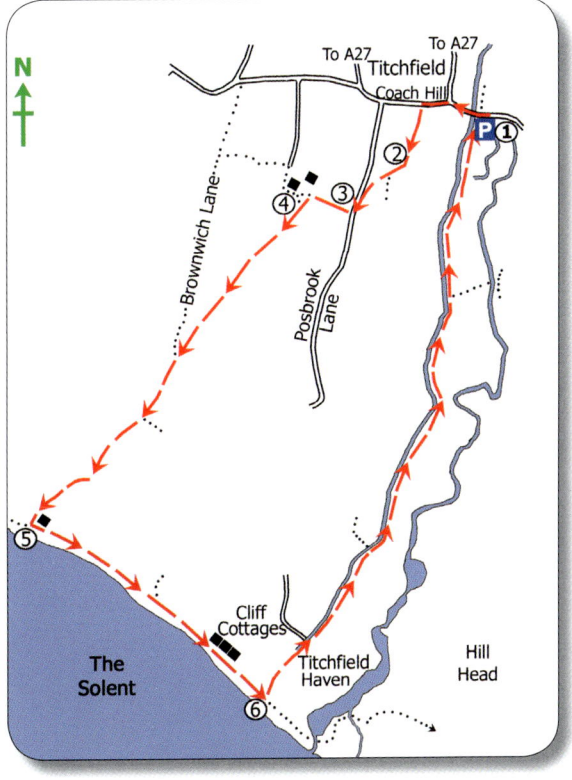

65

River Hamble Country Park

Spike, impatient to be off.

Not only is this a great family walk, ideal if you have younger children with you, but with lovely views over the beautiful Hamble estuary it also makes an enjoyable walk for just you and the dog! Dogs can go off the lead for much of the circuit. There are also a number of places where you can get down to small beaches by the estuary's edge and your dog can swim in the water. The walk is also a great one for socialising older puppies, as there are always plenty of other dogs to meet. There is also a special enclosed doggy exercise and training field (do book at weekends) and a dog washing facility. For family visits, the paths are well surfaced and signposted. There are toilets and two cafés so you are never far from tea, coffee and cake!

The Hamble estuary is internationally important for its biodiversity, particularly the intertidal areas such as the saltmarshes and mudflats you can see from parts of the pathway. On a quiet day watch out for wading birds, cormorants and even the occasional kingfisher. The Hamble estuary is also one of the busiest stretches of water for recreational boating. The woodlands were

River Hamble Country Park 14

once part of the Norman Royal Forest of Bere which stretched across this part of south Hampshire, and timber from the woodlands was later important to fuel the iron works at Funtley and in the shipyards at Bursledon and Warsash.

Terrain
Mostly well-drained woodland tracks and gravel paths through the country park, with one stretch of bridleway which can be a little muddy and rutted. Some minor ascents and descents up and down small slopes and steps, but nothing too taxing.

Where to park
There are numerous car parks within River Hamble Country Park. All are pay and display. For more information on current car parking charges, opening times and more about the park you can visit the website www.hants.gov.uk/thingstodo/countryparks/rhcp. The walk starts from those car parks closest to the entrance – Durncombe Copse, Sandpit Copse, Hoe Moor Copse or Bottom Copse (SU494113–SU496113). There are toilets and a café at Barnfield carpark, and the special dog field plus BBQ pitches are off Toplands car park. All car parks are pay and display. **OS Map:** Explorer 119 Meon Valley, Portsmouthm Gosport and Fareham.

How to get there
River Hamble Country Park is near Botley and Hedge End. It is just a few minutes from Junction 8 of the M27 and signposted from there. The entrance is from Pylands Lane, off Dodwell Lane. Sat Nav: SO31 1BH.

Nearest refreshments
There are two cafes on or near the route, the Barn Café at Barnfield which is just 500 yards or so from the start/end point, and the Farm Café is half way around the walk. There are bookable BBQ pitches if you wanted to bring your

Dog factors
Distance: 3½ miles
Road walking: The route crosses the park's access road in a few places, and a track leading to a handful of properties.
Livestock: None directly on the route, although there are sheep in one of the fields behind a sturdy fence.
Stiles: None
Nearest vets: Adelaide Vetinary Centre, Bursledon.

Hampshire & the New Forest

own or pubs a short drive away in Hedge End, Botley or Bursledon. The Jolly Sailor (☎ 023 8040 5557) is a five-minute drive, a lovely pub overlooking the Hamble; located just off the A27 at Bursledon (GR: SU490094). It is easiest to park up at Bursledon station and walk around to the pub.

The Walk

1 Exit the carpark to the right to find an offroad pathway which runs parallel to the entrance road behind the carparks. Turn left onto this path and go downhill, ignoring further paths back to other carparks to the left or crossings of woodland paths. Keep going downhill until you cross a wide gravel path waymarked '**Strawberry trail**'. Turn right here and after a few minutes you will start to see the **River Hamble** ahead. Ignore the bridge and Strawberry Trail waymarkers to the right, and continue along the pathway, enjoying the estuary views, to the small pontoon.

Do bear in mind that the mud around the estuary is very thick. There are also other places where dogs can play in the water such as the pontoon or small beaches further along the route which are less muddy!

2 After the pontoon the paths diverge and rejoin in various places. There is a woodland route and various diversions that run closer to the estuary. This route follows the estuary where possible. Take the steps down to the right following the estuary, signposted '**Strawberry Trail**', and then keep to the right, following the estuary line. Ignore paths to the left, and cross over a small creek, using the wooden bridge. At a crossing of paths again keep to the right. After crossing another bridge there is another fork in the woodland paths on the slope ahead. This time continue straight on into the woodland following signs for the **Strawberry Trail**. After a few hundred yards the path moves out of the woodland into a field, with views over the estuary valley to the right. Continue along the field boundary for 100 yards or so to a wide gap in the hedge to the left next to a large single tree.

3 Pass left through the gap, and continue straight on along the wide pathway between fields to a kissing gate and junction of paths. The main car park for **Manor Farm** is located here *so you may want to put your dog on a lead at this point on busy days*. If you fancy refreshments you can continue straight on through the gate to the **Farm Café**. If not turn left and follow the wide pathway straight on running parallel with the park's access road.

4 As the path turns to the left, just before a large gate, pass through the wide gap in the hedge, cross the road, and continue straight on up a bridleway. This exits the park, and passes several properties on the left hand side. After

River Hamble Country Park 14

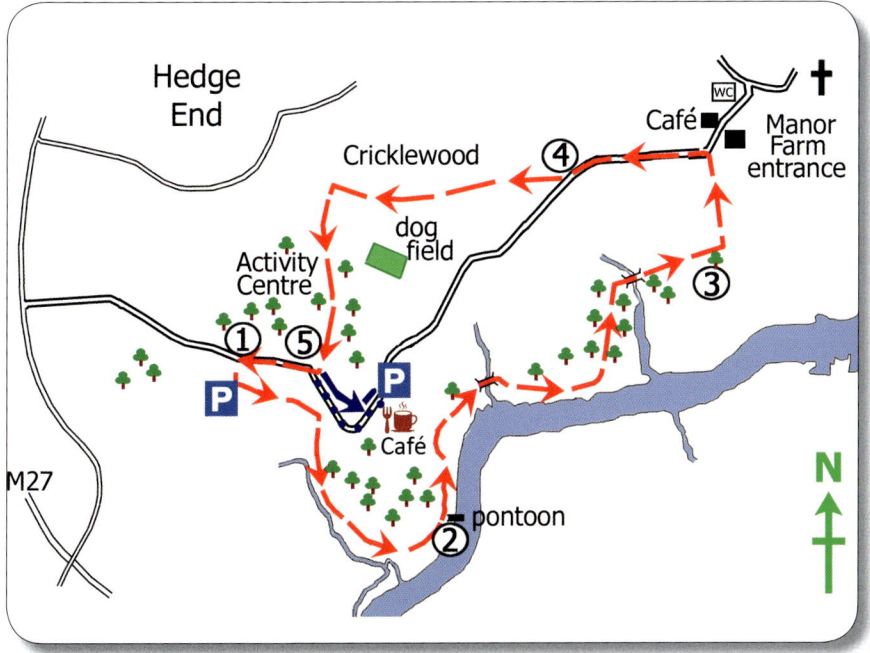

passing **King's Copse Farm** and **Hill Top Cottage**, start looking out for a footpath to the left, just past **Cricklewood**. Pass through the gap and continue between fields, entering back into the country park.

If you want to take a look at the special dog exercise field, take the small woodland path to the left on entering the park and follow this round to the field. You can rejoin the main access route via Toplands car park or follow one of the other woodland routes to get back to the car.

5 To get back to the car continue straight on through the woodland until you pass the Barnfield play area and café, where the path becomes tarmac and you soon reach the main access route. Turn right to return to your car park, or if the park is busy you can find the parallel track again behind the carparks for a car-free route.

Lepe Loop

Lepe Beach.

A **coastal walk** along a pretty and varied stretch of pebbly beach on the New Forest National Park coastline. Dogs can go off lead and play in the sea along the beach, while you beachcomb or enjoy great views across to the Isle of Wight and watch life on the Solent go by. The walk is relatively flat, and well signposted in an easy to navigate rectangular loop, returning through some of Lepe's fertile coastal farmland. You could make a day of it in the adjacent Lepe Country Park, where there is a special doggy beach, and plenty of history. Lepe was a major departure point for troops, vehicles and supplies for the 1944 D-Day landings, and a construction site for part of the prefabricated floating Mulberry harbour. It is a much more tranquil spot these days though, and much of the coastline is of European importance for its biodiversity, particularly gulls, waders, and seabirds such as cormorants, so do bring your binoculars.

Terrain

Flat along the beach, with the pathway a little rough in places. The farmland is

Lepe Loop (15)

> ## Dog factors
> **Distance:** 4½ miles.
> **Road walking:** A ¼ mile of road walking, mostly on pavements on top of the sea defences at Lepe, plus a hundred yards or so along a quiet coastal road – although there can be more through traffic on hot sunny days.
> **Livestock:** Ponies after point 5, and some of the fields around point 3 may be grazed at certain times of the year, plus llamas at point 4.
> **Stiles:** None.
> **Nearest vets:** Seadown Veterinary Group, Hythe.

also relatively flat, with some very gentle slopes. The route is well waymarked from Lepe and the rectangular route is easy to navigate barring a few bends and turns around point 3 and 4 and meetings of paths.

Where to park
The pay and display car park at Lepe Country Park (GR: SZ455985). **OS map:** Explorer OL22 New Forest.

How to get there
Lepe Country Park is well signposted, and lies to the south of Hythe and Fawley. It is accessed from the north via the A326, which runs between Totton and Fawley, then is signposted from Holbury through Blackfield. From the west, cross the river at Beaulieu and follow signs for Exbury Gardens, then on to Lepe. Sat Nav: SO45 1AD

Nearest refreshments
There is a nice café at the country park, The Lookout, which is dog friendly. It serves main meals as well as snacks and hot drinks. You can also hire your own BBQ if you book ahead. The website www.hants.gov.uk/lepe gives café opening times and more information (☎ 02380 899108).

The Walk

1 Facing the sea, turn right out of the car park and along the pavement and sea defences. As the road bends slightly to the right, continue straight on along a gravel path to the back of the white cottage. Continue along past groynes,

Hampshire & the New Forest

passing in front of **Lepe House**. Ignore the first pathway back up to the road, and continue along the beach when the gravel path stops. Continue past a marshy area. There is a distinct pathway between the marsh and the bank, in front of **Inchmery House**. Eventually the path and road join together again. *With dogs on leads*, exit the beach onto the road, and turn left, leaving the coastline. Pass **Shepherds** and **Threestones**.

❷ On the corner of the bend in the road, turn right along the footpath via a kissing gate, leading to a wooded pathway between fields. Pass over a boardwalk, and the path bends to the right through a wooded meadow and over a small stream. Continue over a second small stream and, emerging into an open field, the path bends to the left. Keep to the field boundary with woodland on your left. The path soon bends to the left again just after a small narrow field flanked by a large hedgerow. Keep this hedgerow to your left, and continue straight up the field. The path then curves to the right through a gap in the field. Continue straight on, ignoring an unsigned path to the left and a footpath to the right.

❸ At the end of the field at a T-junction of paths turn to the right, keeping the fenceline and a large arable field to the left and a pasture field and woodland to the right. Gradually a house ahead becomes more and more visible. *There*

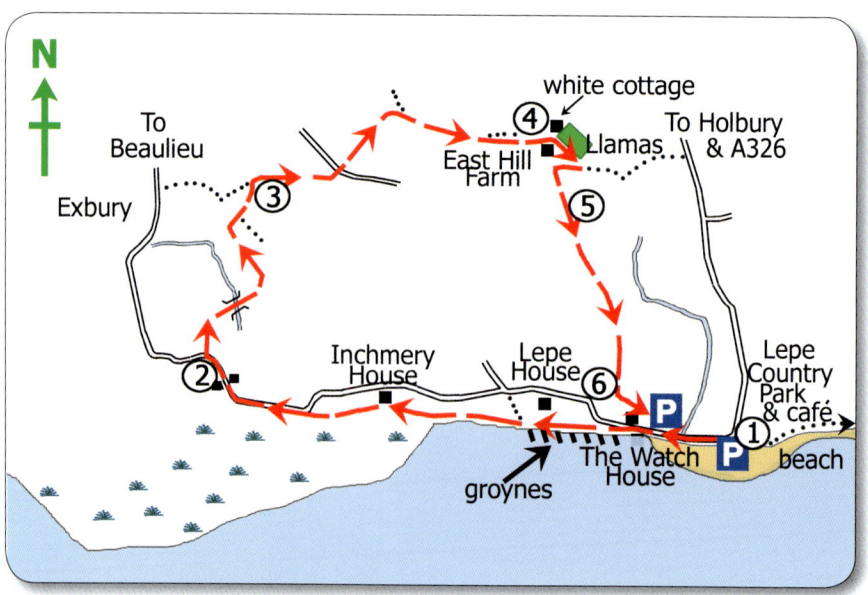

72

Lepe Loop 15

is a road crossing point beyond the house, so dogs need to go on leads before you reach it. Cross the road and continue up a waymarked gravel driveway, enjoying views across the fields to the coastline, until you reach the buildings of a large house – **East Hill Farm**.

4 *With dogs on leads*, keep on the driveway past the white cottage to your left. Just past the cottage, look out for a waymarked footpath straight on, past a field of llamas! The paths starts going downhill slightly at a large oak into a woodland. At a T-junction of paths turn right, then follow this path round to the left and out of the woodland through a gap.

5 This straight path leads back to the coast and the car. *It mainly crosses farmland, and there are some ponies en route, so dogs need to be under close control.* Cross the middle of the large arable field ahead and a smaller field. Continue straight on between arable and pasture fields with woodland and then enter a grazed pasture via a kissing gate. Keep to the fenceline, then continue straight on through the large gap ahead.

6 Cross over a ditch in the next field, then head for the top left-hand corner to a double gate into the next field. Aim diagonally left to the trees to the back of the houses, and then exit through a gate into a gravel overflow car park for **Lepe**. Turn left onto the road and continue back to the car.

Barton Explorer

Spike on the beach at Beckton Bunny.

Barton has one of Hampshire's few beaches, still pebbly, but good for both human and canine swimming and a popular summer destination. With beautiful sea views out to the Needles, it is also a great walk on a winter's day to blow away the cobwebs, before heading to one of the seafront cafés for a slap-up cream tea. This unashamedly short and leisurely loop gives you plenty of opportunities to explore Barton's cliffs and beaches in your own time; come and spend the day at the seaside!

The walk starts at the eastern end of Barton's clifftop promenade, heads along the clifftops, through the clifftop golf course to Barton Common and then returns to the promenade. If you have plenty of energy left, there are miles of the clifftops left to explore. If you wanted to spend time on the beach you can get down to it from a pathway next to the Beachcomber café. It is not advisable to venture too far off the beaten track along the beaches to Beckton (Becton) Bunny or Highcliffe, without checking the tide timetables however, as the high tide could cut you off.

Barton Explorer 16

Terrain
The walk uses well-trodden permissive coastal pathways, and returns on rights of way through a golf course, Barton Common and a small wood. An entirely flat route, and paths are unlikely to be too muddy in winter.

Where to park
There are numerous pay and display car parks along the seafront, plus free roadside parking most of the way along Marine Drive. The walk starts from Marine Drive East pay and display car park (GR: SZ240925). **OS map:** OL22 New Forest.

How to get there
Barton is signposted from the A337 between Lymington and Christchurch. Sat Nav: BH25 7DU

Nearest refreshments
The nearest café is the Beachcomber, a short stroll along the clifftops in Barton, but there are others further along too. The Beachcomber has water and a tethering spot outside specially for dogs and, although Spike and I preferred to sit outside to soak up the sun in the garden area, dogs are allowed inside too. The café serves main meals as well as cakes and hot drinks. ☎ 01425 611599.

The Walk

① From the car park find the cliff top walk and set off with the sea on your right hand side. On reaching a second car park, take the gate on your left-hand side as you face the sea, and continue along the clifftops, enjoying the sea views. *Do be very cautious of the cliff edge. Dogs may need to be on the lead if, like Jack Russell puppy Spike, they have no sense of danger whatsoever!*

Dog factors
Distance: 2 miles (plus miles of walk extensions to explore at your leisure).
Road walking: A few hundred yards along suburban roads, on pavements.
Livestock: None, but you will meet plenty of other people and dogs.
Stiles: None
Nearest vets: Forest Lodge Veterinary Practice, New Milton.

Hampshire & the New Forest

2 After 500 yds or so the path forks. Take the left-hand fork down into the line of scrub, and across a narrow gully, called **Beckton Bunny**.

If you have time, you can walk a few yards further along the coast path to access the Beckton Bunny gully, where it is possible to pick your way down to the sea, a beautiful picnic site, and a lovely spot for your dog to play in the sea. It is also possible to walk for miles along the clifftops and back for a more strenuous walk.

To continue the loop, turn left almost immediately into the golf course, following the well-defined right of way flanked by gorse running diagonally to the left. Ignore any crossing golf buggy tracks and continue along the right of way.

3 Exit the golf course via the kissing gate onto **Barton Common** and follow the line of gorsey scrub straight on. At the fork, take the left-hand path, skirting the back of the golf course. The scrub opens out into grassland, and you'll start to see the houses of **Barton** towards the top of the common. Continue diagonally across to the small car park at the entrance to the common.

4 Do not exit into Barton; instead take the woodland pathway at the bottom left-hand corner of the car park. Continue through the copse until you skirt the backs of houses. *Put dogs on a lead here as you exit onto the road*. Turn left into **Becton Lane**, and continue along the pavement until you reach Marine Drive East. Turn right to return to your car park.

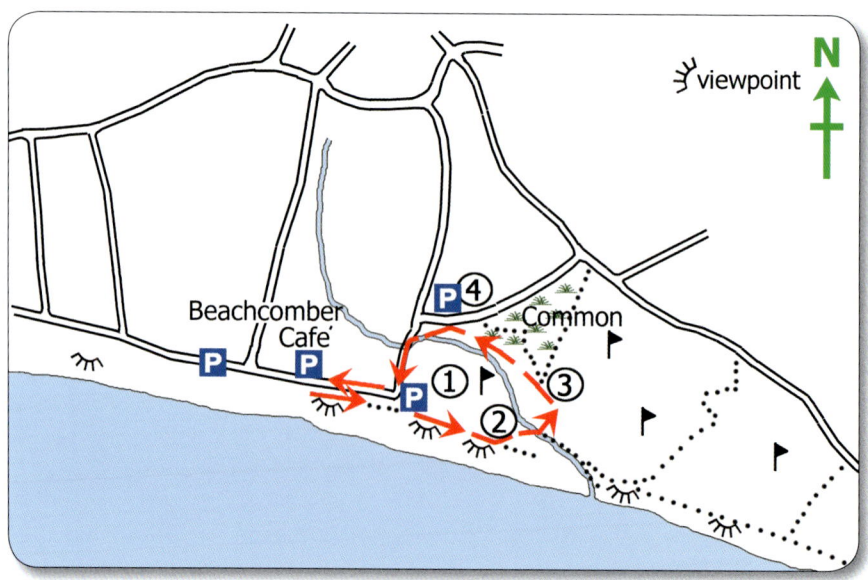

Rhinefield to Wilverley Plain

New Forest ponies grazing on Wilverley Plain.

A **classic New Forest walk** taking in ornamental woodlands, wide expanses of heath, a pony-grazed lawn and stunning views. There are several streams in which your dog can play. The initial approach along the Rhinefield Ornamental Drive past giant redwoods, Douglas firs and lofty spruces, and Rhinefield House (a huge Victorian mock Gothic-cum-Tudor pile) is all part of the experience. This is one of the more challenging walks due to its remoteness and terrain and you'll certainly feel like you've stretched your legs!

Hampshire & the New Forest

Terrain
Uses paths and tracks through heathlands and woodlands, so a back-up OS map is a must. Whilst most streams are crossed by bridges, you might find muddy or boggy patches in winter and after heavy rain, particularly between points 3 to 4 and 5 to 6. There are no steep rises or descents.

Where to park
Puttles Bridge Forestry Commision car park (free), off the Rhinefield road (GR: SU270029). **OS map:** Explorer OL22 New Forest.

How to get there
From Lyndhurst take the A35 towards Christchurch. After Bank and signs for the Reptile Centre, watch out for a sharp left-hand bend, and then turn left at a crossroads, following brown signs for Rhinefield House and Rhinefield Ornamental Drive. The car park is on the left after Rhinefield House. Sat Nav: SO42 7QB

Nearest refreshments
There are no refreshment stops on the walk but you will find several nice spots along the route for a picnic. Alternatively, Brockenhurst and Lyndhurst are not far away, with numerous pubs and cafés. The delightful (and popular) Oak Inn at Bank is certainly worth a visit and is dog- and walker-friendly (☎ 023 8028 2350).

The Walk

1 Take the wide gravel path at the end of the car park, signposted '**Ober Water**'. Almost immediately take the wide grassy path to the left, into the **Aldridgehill Inclosure**. At a crossroads of paths with a wider vehicle track, turn left, and

Dog factors
Distance: 5 miles.
Road walking: None, but crosses forest roads in several places.
Livestock: Ponies and occasional cattle between points 2 and 7. Breeding birds on the heathlands mean your dog should be kept close or on a lead between March and July.
Stiles: None.
Nearest vets: Midforest Veterinary Practice, Lyndhurst.

Rhinefield to Wilverley Plain ⑰

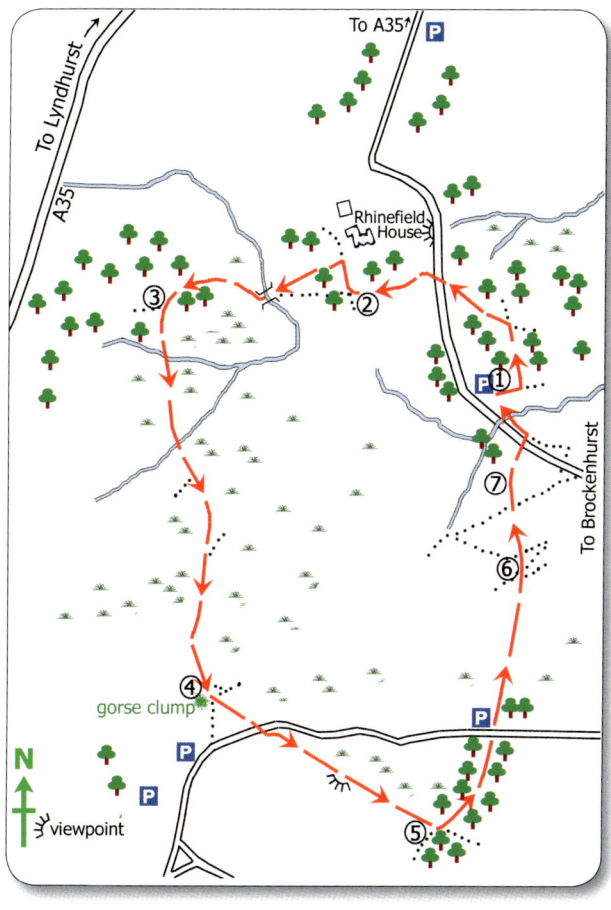

continue straight along this track until you reach the road. Cross over the road and enter the woodland opposite via the wooden Forestry Commission gate. *The road is a minor one, but can be busy at weekends, so dogs need to go on leads to cross the road.*

❷ After 500 yards or so at a crossroads of paths, take the right-hand path through a gate to see views of the back of **Rhinefield House**. Turn left away from the house through the brackeny woodland glade towards the heathland beyond the inclosures. Pass over a small footbridge, heading for the larger bridge straight ahead. *Dogs can cool off on hot days and have a play in the wide stream here whilst you enjoy the views. It is also a very nice picnic spot.* Continue straight on along the distinct track towards the woodland at the top of the slight rise. Follow the path between the two woodlands, until you reach a crossroads of wide forest paths.

❸ Turn left out onto the open heath, following a distinct and wide track through the middle of **Hincheslea Moor** with beautiful views across the Forest. Cross over two streams as the path gradually rises, ignoring a few criss-crossing forest tracks. After a mile the path emerges from the heathland onto **Wilverley Plain**, a classic New Forest lawn grazed by ponies. Continue straight on along the edge of the lawn, until you reach the bottom left-hand corner.

Hampshire & the New Forest

4 The paths start to diverge at a large gorse clump. Ignore a small track to the left of the clump, but as the edge of the lawn curves round to the right take the diagonal left-hand track towards the road. *Dogs should go on a lead here, as the minor road can get busy at peak visitor times.* Cross the road, and continue straight on along the path opposite, still heading diagonally left. Head for **Hincheslea Wood** straight ahead, ignoring crossing paths and continuing for about a further ½ mile.

5 On the woodland edge you will come across a fork in the path. Take the left-hand fork, continuing along the woodland edge, back towards the road. *Dogs back on a lead for a few minutes to cross.* Go over the road, through the **Hincheslea car park** and back onto **Hincheslea Moor** on a distinct wide grassy track.

6 After a slight rise to **Red Hill**, the heather turns to higher gorse and there is a profusion of paths. Ignore the first criss-crossing path; at a fork take the diagonal-left track. Ignore another criss-crossing path and continue straight on. As you come down off the rise you should be able to see the mixed woodland of **Aldridgehill Inclosure** in the mid-distance, the minor road running in front of it, and (if you have good eyesight) a Forestry Commission car park sign on the road to the right. Ignore another criss-crossing path and continue down towards the trees and the road beyond.

7 On the approach to the clump of trees, take the left-hand track onto the road. Cross over onto the gravel track running parallel to the road, and turn left into the woodland. Cross over the stream; the car park is directly ahead. *The Ober Water presents a perfect opportunity at the end of a long walk for your dog to have a drink and cool off, whilst you enjoy some refreshment.*

Visitors enjoying Aldridgehill Inclosure.

Smugglers' Road

Spike surveying the heathland in the Forest.

A **shorter New Forest walk,** which packs in great views from the intriguingly-named Smugglers' Road. Dogs can go off the lead for most of the year on this car-free route, and there is a conveniently placed stream halfway round to cool off in summer or have a play in. The walk starts off on broad and well-used paths along a ridgeline with views of the Forest on both sides, and returns on quieter tracks through heathland. The area is of international importance for biodiversity, as the heathlands support a wide range of rare plants and animals, such as the insect-eating sundew plants, specialist birds, and reptiles such as adders and grass snakes. New Forest ponies are also commonly spotted along this route.

The New Forest was associated with smuggling in the 18th century. Quiet inlets along the rural coastline provided perfect landing points for contraband, and the wilds of the Forest perfect cover for transporting the goods into neighbouring towns. Burley was particularly associated with smuggling, and the Smugglers' Road, criss-crossed with smaller paths, was reputedly

Hampshire & the New Forest

constructed to transport smuggled goods under cover of night. A cottage just off the route, Knaves Ash, was the home of a smuggling family, the Warnes. Legend has it that the wonderfully-named Lovey Warne would parade across Vereley Hill in a red cloak to warn smugglers on the coast if government men were in the area on the lookout.

Terrain

The walk starts off on a wide and well-defined Forest path along a ridgeline, but uses narrower paths, which are a bit rougher, on the way back through the heathland. The walk is one of the easier New Forest walks to navigate though, in a there-and-back loop. The ground is sandy and well drained most of the year round, but likely to be boggy in places in the winter.

Where to park

Smugglers' Road, a free Forestry Commission car park (GR: SU188040). **OS map:** Explorer OL22 New Forest.

How to get there

Just 5 minutes from the A31, off the road to Burley. Burley is signposted from the A31, accessible from either direction. You are likely to spot the service stations well before the turn. Follow signs to Burley south into the Forest. After the Vereley Hill car park start watching out for a signpost to Crow and Moortown on the right-hand side. Take this road downhill; the car park is on the right after a further ½ mile. Sat Nav: BH24 4HQ

Nearest refreshments

None on the route, so do take your own and sit and enjoy the views. There are several pubs and cafés in Burley. Many of the pubs in the village are also associated with smuggling. A secret cellar was discovered in the 17th-

Dog factors

Distance: 2½ miles.
Road walking: None.
Livestock: You are likely to encounter New Forest ponies and domestic horses and their riders. Please also note that this is a heathland walk so dogs should be on a lead or under close control on the path between March and July to avoid disturbance to ground nesting birds.
Stiles: None.
Nearest vets: Cedar Veterinary Group, Ringwood.

Smugglers' Road

century Queen's Head pub during renovation work, uncovering a stash of pistols, coins and alcohol thought to be left there by local smugglers. Dogs are allowed at The Burley Inn (☎ 01425 403448), The Queen's Head (☎ 01425 403423) and The Old Farmhouse Restaurant (☎ 01425 402218).

The Walk

1 From the car park take the gravel path straight up the hill, lined by gorse and birch trees. At the top, after enjoying the views, turn right and follow the wide pathway, the Smugglers' Road, round onto the open heathland. The path rises gradually, and follows a ridgeline with fantastic views on both sides. Ignore any smaller paths right or left and follow the ridgeline path for around a mile. The path gradually rises to a plateau, and you will be able to see the Burley services and hear the faint sound of the A31.

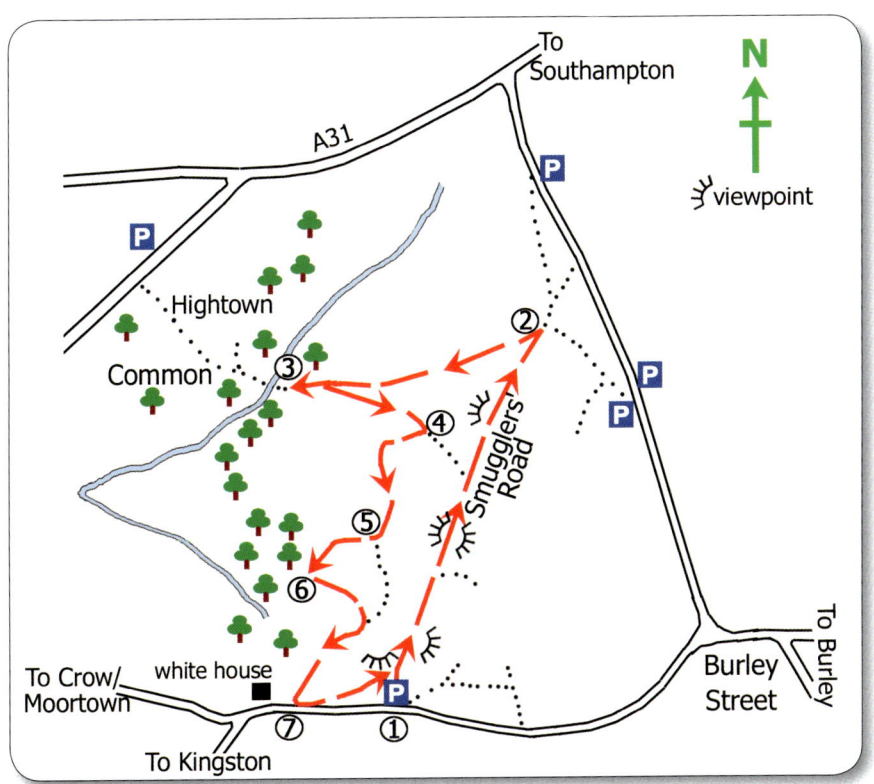

Hampshire & the New Forest

2 After a lone birch tree, a few minutes' walk brings you to an obvious meeting of pathways. Take the path diagonally to the left, almost turning back on yourself. Continue downhill, over a rise, and then heading for the woodland at the bottom of the valley.

3 Enter the trees to find a small stream, and farm on the other side, with tracks continuing onto **Hightown Common**. The open heathland path can be very hot work when the sun is shining, so the stream and woodland will give you and your dog a welcome moment of shade and a splash in the water. To resume the walk, retrace your steps 100 yards or so back up the hill, this time branching off to the right along a narrow 18 ins wide heathland path. There are two forks leading off the main path, which join to form a wider 3 ft wide path. This follows the contours of the hillside through the heathland.

4 At a fork in the path, where one narrow track leads uphill, take the right-hand fork, continuing your way around the curves of the hillside.

5 At a second fork in a dip, again take the right-hand path winding around the hillside, this time skirting fairly close to the heathland edge with woodland to the right.

6 As the path reaches a clump of trees, it joins a wide vehicle track. Turn left onto this track, and continue around the hillside through the heathland. When you spot a white cottage on your right-hand side, **Knaves Ash**, once home to smuggler Lovey Warne, *it might be an idea to put dogs back on the lead if they are off.*

7 At the junction with the road, you can either turn left and follow the road back to the car for 250 yds, or for an off-lead finish take the path on the left-hand side leading back up the hill to the viewpoint, and back down the way you came to the car park.

The Smugglers' Path.

Fritham

New Forest ponies taking a dip at Cadnam's Pool.

An almost entirely off-road walk in the remote northern New Forest. Dogs will enjoy being off the lead. There are interesting scents and smells all the way round, and two ponds (one of them on the longer circuit) for water-loving dogs to play in. Owners meanwhile will enjoy the beautiful Forest scenes of woodlands, wild and remote heathlands, and the two pretty ponds both make great picnic spots. Fritham lies in the heart of the New Forest National Park, a settled enclosure surrounded by traditional grazed woodlands, heathland and several Forest Inclosures planted in the 19th century. The Forest habitats are internationally important for wildlife, so bring the binoculars and enjoy the common sightings of deer and wild ponies.

The surrounding landscape is full of history from Bronze Age bowl barrows (funerary monuments) to evidence of Roman pottery kilns, and a medieval hunting lodge. The beautiful Eyeworth Pond, with its ornamental ducks, wild birds and ponies drinking from the water's edge is no natural feature. It was created in the 1860s by the Schultze Gunpowder Company, based for

Hampshire & the New Forest

many years in nearby Eyeworth Lodge. The remote New Forest location was selected to build the factory to limit potential damage should unexpected explosions occur. It produced smokeless powder for sporting guns. In 1896 the company employed upwards of 100 people in 60 buildings. The factory closed in 1921.

Terrain
The walk is mainly on woodland tracks and pathways, which are not signposted and therefore can be difficult to navigate in places. The pathways are mainly in good condition, but in one or two places may be uneven or boggy. The route is gently undulating rather than hilly, but nonetheless the distance and open Forest terrain make it one of the more challenging in this book.

Where to park
The Forestry Commission free car park on the western edge of Fritham (GR: SU231141). **OS map:** Explorer OL22 New Forest.

How to get there
Fritham lies to the north of the A31 and south of the Cadnam to Fordingbridge road. From Southampton come off the M27 at junction 1 for Cadnam, and take the 3rd exit at the roundabout onto the B3079. Turn left onto the B3078 for Fordingbridge and follow signs off this road for Fritham. From Ringwood you can exit directly from the A31 towards Linwood and Fritham. Sat Nav: SO43 7HL

Nearest refreshments
The Royal Oak in Fritham is dog-friendly, family-friendly and does great food. Busy on summer days. ☎ 023 8081 2606.

Dog factors
Distance: 6 miles, or a shorter circuit of 1½ miles if you return to the car park from point 3.
Road walking: A few hundred yards along a quiet vehicle track.
Livestock: New Forest ponies likely, horses and riders common, and possibility of cattle on heathland areas. Dogs should be under close control in spring and summer months on the heathlands due to ground nesting birds.
Stiles: None.
Cyclists: Likely on the cycle track at point 3
Nearest vets: Midforest Veterinary Practice, West Totton.

Fritham 19

The Walk

1. From the car park, exit towards the road and turn left along the quiet lane. Continue for 500 yds until you come to **Eyeworth Pond**, one of the prettiest sights in the New Forest and a fantastic picnic spot for your return. *Although Poppy a Jack Russell, didn't fancy a dip on this occasion, water-loving dogs can enjoy a swim here.*

2. Continue on the lane past **Eyeworth Lodge** until it runs out at **Oak Tree Cottage**. Ignore the bridleway straight on and bear left on forest tracks,

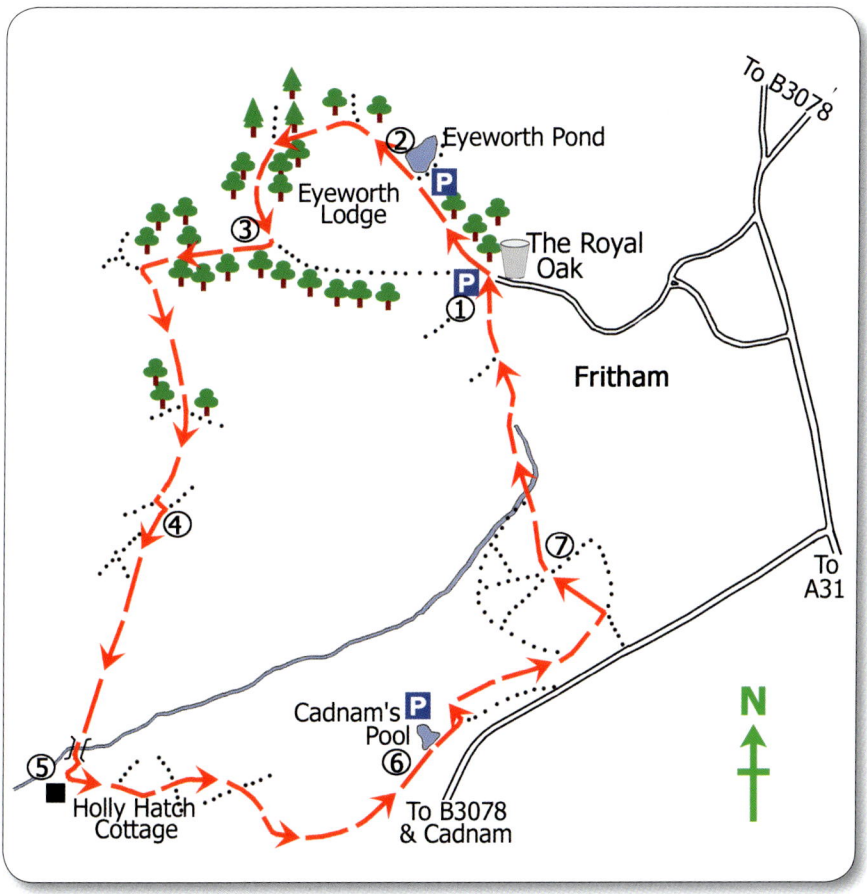

Hampshire & the New Forest

keeping the field boundary in view to the left. When the field boundary swings further left, continue straight on across the earth boundary on a path that takes you between coniferous plantation on the right and deciduous forest to the left. At a T-junction with a wider vehicle track marked by a single large pine, turn left and descend slightly, crossing a small stream, to a gravel cycle track. *Do bear in mind that you will need to share this section of the pathway with cyclists as well as walkers.*

❸ At this point you could turn left and follow the cycle path back to the car park. For the longer walk turn right. Continue along the cycle path until it bears sharply to the right. At this point turn left along a grassy path, which climbs up out of the woodland and emerges onto the open heathland of **Fritham Plain**. Continue straight on, ignoring any tracks to the right and left. As the path enters scrubby woodland, it splits briefly, rejoins, then forks. Take the right-hand fork back into open heathland, heading towards the trees of **Sloden Inclosure**.

❹ At the treeline, continue straight on over a gravel track, ignoring a gate to the right, to a second gravel path with no gate. Turn right along this path into the trees. The path bears slightly to the left, and eventually descends out of the trees to open heath, with beautiful views across the valley to **Holly Hatch Cottage**. Descend towards the cottage.

❺ Cross the bridge, bear right and just before the cottage turn left through a gate into the woodland of **Holly Hatch Inclosure**. At a fork in front of a fenced area of trees take the right-hand fork, ascending through the trees on a grassy path. When you eventually emerge onto a three-way junction of a wide gravel track take the track that leads straight on. Pass through the gate out of the woodland and turn left along a grassy path, which follows the woodland edge for a while then continues through heathland to **Cadnam's Pool**.

Cadnam's Pool is a great place to take a rest; on warm days dogs can cool down in the shallow pool if they like a swim. It can be a magical spot in the quieter months to spot New Forest ponies and other wildlife who come to the pond for a drink.

❻ With the pool on your left, continue along the concrete pathway, and cross over the metalled track leading to the car park. Take a left turn along a grassy path, entering **Anses Wood**. Just inside the woodland turn right along another grassy path. This emerges back out into grassy heathland; the pathway becomes less distinct as the landscape opens out but continue straight on until you come to a gravel track. Turn left down the track, and pass through the gate into a concrete storage area. Continue straight on, heading for the bottom right-hand corner.

Fritham 19

Looking towards Holly Hatch Cottage.

7 Of the two forest paths forking from here, take the left-hand track – which leads you straight on into the woodland. Descend through the woodland (the path here can be rough in places from machinery use), and out through a gate marked '75'. Continue straight on, crossing a small stream (there is no bridge here, but it can be crossed with a good stride) until the path opens out onto a Forest lawn with glimpses of a house on the right. Bear half right, crossing a small stream, across the lawn, aiming for the house, and join the gravel track that runs in front of the property. Turn left and follow the track beside the houses back into the village. The car park is on the left.

Breamore and the Miz-maze

Elizabethan Breamore House.

It is not often that you get to walk so close to one of the nation's finest stately homes, and this route has it all: an Elizabethan manor, a Saxon church, a mysterious sight on a wooded knoll, ancient woodlands, beautiful views over rolling chalk downlands, and one of the most famous stud farms in the country. It could be a scene straight out of a Dick Francis novel! Dogs will need to be on leads through the estate, and under close control through farmland. There are also a few stiles and a short road section. The walk is a good stretch though for both dogs and owners with varied smells and sights – the closest to the West Country that Hampshire gets!

Breamore is within the Cranborne Chase and West Wiltshire Downs Area of Outstanding Natural Beauty, an ancient landscape of woodlands and rolling

Breamore and the Miz-maze 20

chalk hills. The walk starts at Breamore House and Museum, an Elizabethen manor dating from 1583, which overlooks the Avon Valley and New Forest beyond. The Saxon church is also well worth a look, dating from AD 980. Not many churches from this period survived the Norman Conquest in Hampshire. After passing the house and a steady climb through Breamore woodlands, the Miz-maze sits on top of a wooded knoll, enclosed by yew trees. This is one of England's only surviving short-turf mazes, and a suitably atmospheric spot. The rest of the walk is through rolling farmland, with views up to Whitsbury Manor Stud, which has bred a long line of winners over the years – the Grand National winner Desert Orchid spent much of his retirement here.

I have suggested an extension route which takes in Whitsbury Castle hill fort, a 14th century church and the lovely Cartwheel Inn. This is definitely a working landscape though, and some of the other bridleways run straight through the middle of stud farm stables. Do be prepared to share your walk with very expensive horses and put dogs on leads around stud farms. If you fancy making a day of it, Rockbourne Roman Villa is not far away. It is open on Thursdays, Fridays and Sundays from April to September and welcomes dogs on the site. There are also any number of beautiful villages to explore, such as Damerham, Rockbourne and Martin.

Terrain
The walk uses well-trodden bridleways for much of the walk, which mainly have good surfaces although they are rutted in places from farm vehicle use, and can be muddy in winter. There are some steady climbs up and over the downs. The rectangular shape of the walk and clearly marked bridleways makes this route fairly easy to navigate.

Where to park
The free car park at Breamore House and Museum. On quiet days, park directly next to the walled garden (GR: SU151187). On busy summer weekends you may be directed to a nearby field (SU153186). **OS map:** Explorer OL22 New Forest with a small corner on Explorer 130 Salisbury & Stonehenge.

How to get there
Breamore lies north of Fordingbridge in the far west of Hampshire, beyond the New Forest. The A338 from Ringwood to Salisbury runs through Breamore village, and the house and museum are signposted from there. Sat Nav: SP6 2DF

Nearest refreshments
Do check the opening times of the museum and café before you start (☎ 01725 511955; www.breamorehouse.com). If you time your walk right, you can get lunch or drinks there. There are a number of pubs nearby such as

Hampshire & the New Forest

the Bat and Ball in Breamore (☎ 01725 512252). Food is reputedly great and the pub has a bar area where well-behaved dogs are allowed. The Cartwheel Inn in Whitsbury is also worth making a detour for, with good food and real ales, and a friendly welcome for walkers and dogs (☎ 01725 518362).

The Walk

① From the car park, walk past the museum and café towards the church, stopping to explore and admire both the church and views of the house for as long as you wish. To continue the walk, return to point 2.

② The bridleway runs along the driveway to the west of the house itself, and then enters **Breamore Wood**, a bluebell woodland which is very pretty in springtime. *The estate requests that dogs should be on a lead through the woodland.* There is a steady climb through the trees. Take the right-hand fork as the paths divide (clearly marked). The slope eventually levels out and the path emerges into open fields. Do stop to catch your breath and admire the rural views to the left. Follow the track up towards the wooded knoll, ignoring paths to the left and right and stop to explore the Miz-maze.

③ Continue along the ridge behind the Miz-maze knoll, with the field boundary to your right and views over the downs. Ignore the farm track to the left running down beside the knoll but a few yards after that there is a meeting of paths where a footpath crosses the bridleway, with a woodland to the right. Pass over the first stile to the left, taking the footpath down the hill with views over the valley to **Whitsbury Castle and Stud Farm** on the hillside opposite.

Dog factors

Distance: 3½ miles (an extension to Whitsbury from point 4, rejoining the main route at point 5 – adding a total of 2½ miles – is possible; see map).
Road walking: A few hundred yards of quiet village lanes.
Livestock: None directly on the route, but horses and other livestock in nearby fields. Horses in fields may be encountered on the extension.
Stiles: 3, all with gaps in fences underneath or to the side so most dogs should be able to use them, unless larger or less agile. There are further stiles on the extension.
Nearest vets: Forest Veterinary Clinic, Fordingbridge.

Breamore and the Miz-maze

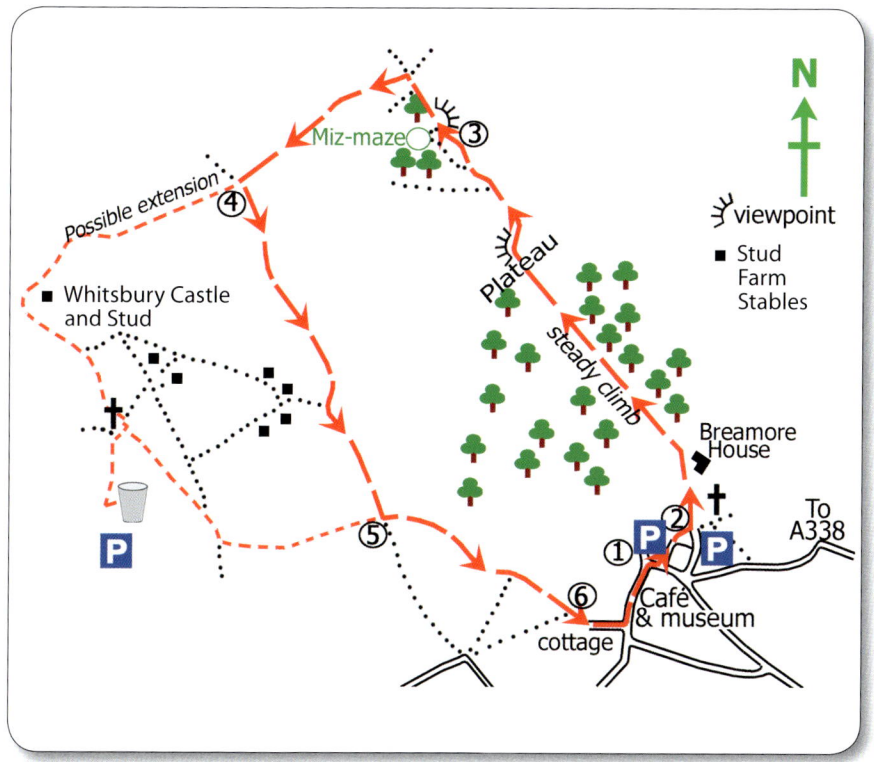

This is an old manor house built on top of an Iron Age hill fort, and now famous for its racehorses.

The path passes through another small woodland and past a barn. Ignore farm tracks to the right and left, continuing straight on down through the woodland to the bottom of the valley. Cross the second stile into the bridleway.

4 Turn left along the bridleway and continue along the bottom of the coombe (dry) for almost a mile. Dogs can go off leads here, although there is likely to be livestock in some of the fields beyond the paths.

5 At a meeting of paths, with a bridleway joining from the right and a footpath signed to the left, turn left onto the footpath – a broad gap between a gate and a hedge. Proceed along the field boundary. Pass over the third stile at the top of the field. Continue along the pathway, which turns into a sunken wooded track between fields. Ignore a bridleway joining from

Hampshire & the New Forest

the right. The path eventually emerges onto Rookery Lane by a very quaint thatched cottage.

6 To return to the car, continue down **Rookery Lane**, turn left at the end and follow the road back to the car park on your left. *These roads are mainly very quiet but it may be worth having dogs on leads if they like to explore, especially on sunny weekends when there is more through-traffic for Breamore House.*

The Saxon church at Breamore.

APPENDIX

Small Animal Veterinary Practices
The following are practices that are close to the walks described.

Adelaide Veterinary Centre
Long Lane, Bursledon, Southampton, SO31 8DA ☎ 023 8040 6215

Alver Veterinary Group
30 Stubbington Green, Stubbington, PO14 2LE ☎ 01329 667551

Amery Veterinary Group
Ashburnham House, Crossways Road, Grayshott, GU26 6HJ ☎ 01428 604442

Ark Veterinary Practice
41 Connaught Road, Fleet, GU51 3LR ☎ 01252 616185

Ashworth Veterinary Group
1 Courtmoor Avenue, Fleet, GU52 7UE ☎ 01252 616136

Cedar Veterinary Group
The Dean, Alresford, SO24 9BH ☎ 01962 732535

Cedar Veterinary Group
69 Christchurch Road, Ringwood BH24 1DH ☎ 01425 473683

Chandlers Ford and Boyatt Wood Veterinary Surgery
47A Winchester Road, Chandlers Ford, SO53 2GF ☎ 023 8025 2543

Companion Care Veterinary Surgery
Pets at Home, 140–148 Southampton Road, Park Gate, Fareham, PO14 4PH
☎ 01489 553704

Firgrove Veterinary Centre
1-3 Aylesham Way, Yateley, GU46 6NR ☎ 01252 877799

Forest Veterinary Clinic
7 Park Road, Fordingbridge, SP6 1EQ ☎ 01425 652221

Forest Lodge Veterinary Practice
14 Barton Court Road, New Milton, BH25 6NP ☎ 01425 614482

Foxcotte Veterinary Group
33 Winchester Street, Whitchurch, RG28 7AJ ☎ 01256 892067

GKG Vets, Kingsclere and Newbury
19 George Street, Kingsclere, RG20 5NH and 43 St Johns Road, Newbury, RG14 7PS ☎ 01635 297557 (Kingsclere) and 01635 40565 (Newbury and emergency out of hours number)

Harbour Veterinary Group
95 St Marys Road, Hayling Island, PO11 9DD ☎ 023 9246 7845

Kynoch Vets (Medivet Yateley)
Forge Court Veterinary Clinic, Reading Road, Yateley, GU46 7RX ☎ 01252 873569

Mainstone Veterinary Clinic
Mainstone, Romsey, SO51 6BA ☎ 01794 513157

Midforest Veterinary Practice, Lyndhurst and West Totton
Glenber Cottage, Beechen Lane, Lyndhurst, SO43 7DD and Kingfisher House, Ringwood Road, West Totton, Hants, SO40 7DY ☎ 02380 282358 (Lyndhurst) and 023 8066 0400 (West Totton)

Orchard Veterinary Surgery
121a The Hundred, Romsey, Hampshire, SO51 8BZ ☎ 01794 830288 or out of hours emergency number ☎ 0845 223 4492

St Peter's Vets
Liss Veterinary Surgery, Mill Road, Liss, GU33 7AZ ☎ 01730 894222

Seadown Veterinary Group
Frost Lane, Hythe, Southampton, SO45 3NG ☎ 023 8084 2237

Shield Veterinary Centre
Victoria Road, Bishops Waltham, Southampton SO32 1DJ ☎ 01489 896734

Stable Close Veterinary Clinic
St Cross Road, Winchester, SO23 9PR ☎ 01962 840505 or 01962 841001

Vets4Pets, Hayling
104-106 Elm Grove, Hayling Island, PO11 9EH ☎ 02392 636950

Walkabout Vet
The Old Coachworks, Station Road, Over Wallop, SO20 8HU ☎ 07957 349985 or 01264 782536